D1550654

TALKS AND DIALOGUES
J. KRISHNAMURTI

 A DISCUS BOOK/PUBLISHED BY AVON BOOKS

AVON BOOKS
A division of
The Hearst Corporation
1790 Broadway
New York, New York 10019

First Avon Printing: January 1970
First Discus Printing: April 1983

DISCUS TRADEMARK REG. U.S. PAT. OFF. AND IN
OTHER COUNTRIES, MARCA REGISTRADA, HECHO EN
CANADA

Printed in Canada

UNV   12 11 10 9 8

TALKS AND DIALOGUES

talks at saanen

1

WE ARE GOING to have ten talks so that we can take things quietly, patiently and intelligently. It behoves those of us who are serious and who have not merely come for one or two talks, out of curiosity to understand the various complications and problems that each human being has, for to understand is to resolve them and be completely free of them.

There are certain things which must be taken for granted. First we must understand what we mean by communication, what the word means to each one of us, what is involved, what is the structure, the nature, of communication. If two of us, you and I, are to communicate with each other there must not only be a verbal understanding of what is being said, at the intellectual level, but also, by implication, listening and learning. These two things, it seems to me, are essential in order that we may communicate with each other, listening and learning. Secondly, each one of us has, obviously, a background of knowledge, prejudice and experience, also the suffering and the innumerable complex issues involved in relationship. That is the background of most of us and with that background we try to listen. After all, each one of us is the result of our culturally complex life—we are the result of the whole culture of man, with the education and the experiences of not only a few years, but of centuries.

I do not know if you have ever examined how you listen, it doesn't matter to what, whether to a bird, to the wind in the leaves, to the rushing waters, or how you listen to a dialogue with yourself, to your conversation in various relationships with your intimate friends, your wife or husband. If we try to listen we find it extraordinarily difficult, because we are always projecting our opinions and ideas, our prejudices, our background, our inclinations, our impulses; when they dominate we hardly listen to what is being said. In that state there is no value at all. One listens and therefore learns, only in a state of attention, a state of silence in which this whole background is in abeyance, is quiet; then, it seems to me, it is possible to communicate.

Several other things are involved. If you listen with the background or image that you may have created about the speaker, and listen as to one with certain authority—which the speaker may, or may not, have—then obviously you are not listening. You are listening to the projection which you have put forward and that prevents you from listening. So again, communication is not possible. Obviously, real communication or communion, can only take place when there is silence. When two people are intent, seriously, to understand something, bringing their whole mind and heart, their nerves, their eyes, their ears, to understand, then in that attention there is a certain quality of silence; then actual communication, actual communion, takes place. In that there is not only learning but complete understanding—and that understanding is not something different from immediate action. That is to say, when one listens without any intention, without any barrier, putting aside all opinions, conclusions—all the rest, experiences—then, in that state one not only understands whether what is being said is true or false, but further, if it is true, there

12

is immediate action, if it is false, there is no action at all.

During these ten talks we are going not only to learn about ourselves, which is of primary importance, but also to learn that in the very process of learning there is action. It is not a matter of learning first and acting afterwards, but rather the very act of learning is the act of doing.

For us, as we are, learning implies the accumulation of ideas—ideas being rationalized and carefully worked-out thought. As we learn we formulate a structure of ideas and having established a formula of ideas, ideals or conclusions, then we act. So there is action separate from idea. This is our life—we formulate first and then try to act according to that formulation. But we are concerned with something entirely different, which is, that the act of learning *is* action; that in the very process of learning action is taking place and that therefore, there is no conflict.

I think it is important to understand from the very beginning that we are not formulating any philosophy, any intellectual structure of ideas or of theological or purely intellectual concepts. We are concerned with bringing about in our lives a total revolution which has nothing whatever to do with the structure of society as it is. On the contrary, unless we understand the whole psychological structure of society of which we are part, which we have put together through centuries, and are entirely free from that structure, there can be no total psychological revolution—and a revolution of that kind is absolutely essential.

You must know what is taking place in the world; of the enormous discontent boiling over and expressing itself in different ways—of the hippies, the beatniks, the provos in America—and of the wars going on, for which we are responsible. It is not only the Americans and the Vietnamese, but each one of us, who are responsible for those monstrous wars—and we are not using the word "responsible" casually. We are responsible, whether they take place in the Middle East, or in the Far East, or anywhere else. There is great starvation going on, inefficient government and the piling up of armaments, and so on. Observing all this, one demands, naturally and humanly, that there must

13

be change, that there must be a revolution in the way of our thinking and living. When is that revolution to begin? It has always been thought by the Communists, by the Nationalists, by all organized religious authorities, that the individual doesn't matter at all; the individual can be persuaded in any direction. Though they assert common freedom for man, they do everything to prevent that freedom. The organized religions throughout the world brain-wash people to make them conform to a particular pattern, which they call religious ideas and rituals. The Communists, the Capitalists, the Socialists are not concerned with the individual at all, although they talk about him; but I don't see how a radical change can come about except through the individual. For the individual human being is the result of the total experience, knowledge and conduct of man—it is in us. We are the storehouse of all the past, the racial, the family, the individual's experience of life—we are that, and unless in the very essence of our being there is a revolution, a mutation, I do not see how a good society can come about.

When we talk about the individual, we are not opposing him to, or setting him against, the collective, the mass, the whole of mankind, because the human individual *is* the whole of mankind. Unless you feel that, such a statement becomes merely an intellectual concept. Unless each one of us recognizes the central fact that we as individual human beings represent the whole of mankind, whether they live in the Orient or the Occident, we shall not see how to act.

We human beings, as individuals, are totally responsible for the state of the world. Wars—we are responsible for wars by the way we lead our lives, for we are nationalistic, German, French, Dutch, English, American, Russian; we are Catholics, Protestants, Jews, Buddhists, belonging to Zen or this or that sect, dividing, quarrelling, fighting each other. Our gods, our nationalities, have divided us. When one realizes, not intellectually but actually, as actually as you would recognize that you are hungry, that you and I as human beings are responsible for all this chaos, for all this misery—because we contribute to it, we are part of it—

14

when one realizes that, not emotionally, not intellectually, not sentimentally, but actually, then the problem becomes tremendously serious. When that realization has become so serious, you will act. Not until then, not until you feel that you are completely responsible for this monstrous society, with its wars, with its divisions, with its ugliness, brutalities, greeds, and so on, not until each one of us realizes that, will we act. And you can only act when you know how this structure, not only outwardly, but inwardly, has been put together. That is why one must know more about oneself and the more one knows about oneself the more mature one is. Immaturity lies only in one's ignorance of oneself.

What we are going to do is to learn about ourselves—not according to the speaker, or to Freud, or to Jung, to some analyst or philosopher—but to learn actually what we are. If we learn about ourselves according to Freud we learn about Freud, not about ourselves. To learn about oneself, all authority must come to an end, *all authority*—whether it be the authority of the church or of the local priest, or of the famous analyst, or of the greatest philosophers with their intellectual formulas, and so on. So the first thing that one has to realize when we become serious, demanding a total revolution within the structure of our own psyche, is that there is no authority of any kind. That is very difficult, for there is not only the outward authority, which one can easily reject, but there is inward authority; the inward authority of one's own experience, of one's own accumulated knowledge, of the opinions, ideas, ideals which guide one's life and according to which one tries to live. To be free of that authority is immensely difficult— authority, not only in great things, but in the authority of yesterday when you had an experience which taught you something; what it taught becomes the authority of today. Do please understand this, the subtlety, the difficulty of it. There is not only the authority of accumulated knowledge as tradition, of every experience that has left a mark, but there is yesterday's authority which is as destructive as the authority of a thousand years. To understand ourselves

15

needs no authority of yesterday, or of a thousand years, because we ourselves are a living thing, moving, never resting, always flowing. When we look at ourselves with the authority of yesterday, what is important is the authority and not the movement of life which we are, so we don't understand the movement, the flow, the beauty and the quality of that movement—what you understand is the authority you have accumulated, that with which you are examining, looking. To be free of that authority is to die to everything of yesterday so that your mind is always fresh, always young, innocent, full of vigor and passion—it is only in that state that one observes and learns. Such freedom is no longer an instrument to be used by authority according to our pleasure and pain. And for this is required a great deal of awareness, actual awareness of what is going on within the skin, without correcting it, without telling it what it should be, or what it should not be; because if you correct it you have already established the authority, the censor.

If you are willing, serious, and not merely casual and curious, then we will go into it, step by step, not missing a single movement. This doesn't mean that the speaker is going to become the analyst, there is no analyzer and no one to be analyzed, there is only the fact, there is only that which is. When we know how to look at that which is, then the analyzer comes to an end, totally.

So, in these talks, we are going to communicate with each other, not about what should be, or what has been, but about what is actually taking place in us—not about how we should alter it, or what we should do with it, but how to observe and see what actually is. That demands such intense energy! You know, we never look at that which is—we never look at the tree as it is, the shadows, the depth of the foliage, as it is, totally—at the beauty of it. This is because we have concepts of what beauty is and we have formulas of how we should look at the tree, or we want to identify ourselves with it—we have an idea about the tree first and see the tree after. The idea, formula, or ideal, prevents us from looking at the tree that is. Ideas,

16

formulas, ideals comprise the culture in which we live—that culture is me, is you and with that culture we look, therefore there is no looking at all. Now, if you are *listening* to what is being said, actually listening, then the culture, the authority, will totally disappear—you haven't got to fight that background, that culture of the society in which one is brought up—you will be able to recognize that that thing is preventing you from looking. It is only when you actually look that you are in communion, then you have the right contact, not only with the tree, with the cloud, with the mountain, with the beauty of the earth, but also you have direct contact with what is actually within yourself, and when you are directly in contact there is no problem whatever. It is only when there is no contact, when you are the "observer" and the thing observed is something different from you and therefore there is no contact, that the problems arise—then there are the conflicts, the sorrows, pains and anxieties.

During these talks we are going to help each other to understand and therefore to be in contact with what actually is; this means the "observer" comes to an end and that to look, to listen, to understand and to act, are all the same.

Can we talk over together that which we have been saying—or anything else you like? I think it is very important to ask questions, not only ask questions of another but also ask questions of ourselves. We never ask a fundamental question or when we do ask, we have not the time or the inclination, or the capacity to find the right answer. One must be very serious to ask. The more the question becomes intense the more the answer is not to be found; if one is serious, in the very asking of the question you have the answer. But you have to ask.

Questioner: I don't understand this business of immediate action.

KRISHNAMURTI: What is action? The actual meaning of that word is "to do." Action implies an active present. But

17

action is the result of yesterday's mannerisms, knowledge, experience, ideas, formulas, which have become established and we act according to them. The memory of yesterday, modified and so on, acts in the present and that creates the future, so in that action there is no active present. I am acting in accordance with a dead thing. (Of course I must have memory in certain categories of activities, technical and so on.) But acting according to memory only produces action that it not action at all, it is a dead thing, therefore tomorrow is also a dead thing. So what am I to do? I must learn about action which is totally different from the action of memory. To do this I must see what actually takes place, not intellectually, not verbally, not sentimentally. I have had an experience of anger or of pleasure and that remains as a memory, and according to that memory action takes place. That action from memory increases the anger or the pleasure and it is always accumulating the past—such action from the past is virtually inaction. Can the mind be free from these memories of yesterday so as to live in the present? This must not be a question to which I can obtain an intellectual answer. Nor can the mind, which is of time, which is subject to infinite moods, free itself from the memories of yesterday by trying to live in the present in accordance with the philosophy which says "I must live completely in the present" which says "there is no future, there is no past, that the future is hopeless therefore live in the present and make the best of the present."

I cannot live in the present if the present is in the shadow of the past. To understand this the mind must be capable of looking and you can only look when there is no condemnation, no identification, no judgment—as you can look at a tree, a cloud—simply look at it. Before you can look at the most complex structure of memory, you must be able to look at a tree, at the ant, at the movement of the river, to look—we really don't. It is far more important to look at the past as memory, and this we don't know how to do.

Action according to memory, is total inaction, and therefore there is no revolution at all.

Questioner: *I wonder if there is a contradiction between your saying that the individual is the collective and the result of the past and your saying that there must be no authority from the past?*

KRISHNAMURTI: After all, the past, whether invested in another, as in the priest, the analyst, the commander of an army or the wife or the husband, that authority invested by me in another is for my own security, for my own safety. That authority man has accepted for centuries upon centuries. But he has built the authority, he wants the authority, because the more he is confused, the more miserable, the more he wants to have another tell him what to do. The authority which he has invested in another, or the authority which he has created in himself as a guide, becomes an impediment. You see again, this question of authority and the individual is really a very complex affair. To understand the individual we have to understand the collective, and in the collective lies the whole structure of authority. All of us are seeking security in some form or another. Security in jobs, security in having money, security in the continuity of a certain pleasure, sexual or otherwise, and the demand for total security, that is in all of us, and we try to find expression of that urge in different ways. The moment there is the demand for security then there must be authority—obviously—and that is the psychological and cultural structure of our whole society.

Have we ever asked whether this security that we seek, exists at all? We take it for granted it does. We have sought security through churches, through political leaders, through relationships but have we ever found it—have you? Have you ever found security in your relationships? Is there security in any relationship, in any church, or in any government, except physical security? You have security in belief, in dogmas, but that is merely an idea which can be shattered by argument, by doubt, by questioning, by demanding freedom. When one realizes, not as an idea, that there is no such thing as security, permanency, then authority has no meaning whatsoever.

Questioner: I think you said that we are responsible for the whole of society. I have not interpreted exactly what you mean. Are we responsible for the wars and so on?

KRISHNAMURTI: Don't you think that we are responsible for the wars? The way of our lives indicates that we are brutal, aggressive and have violent prejudices, we have divided ourselves into nationalities, religious groups, hating each other, we destroy each other in business; all that must express itself in wars, in hatred—obviously. To live in peace means to live peacefully every day, doesn't it?

Questioner: I would say that some people are more responsible than others.

KRISHNAMURTI: Ah! The gentleman says that some people are more responsible for these uglinesses than you and I. That is a nice, happy way out of it. But I am afraid we are not—when you are a German and I a Russian, when you are a Communist and I am a Capitalist, are we not at each other's throats—are we not antagonistic to each other? You want everything as it is, undisturbed, because you have a little money, a child, a house and for God's sake you don't want to be disturbed—anything that disturbs you, you hate. Are you not responsible when you insist that you will not be disturbed? And you say "my religion, my Buddha, my Christ," my whatever it is, he is my God, in him you have invested everything, your whole security and misery—you don't want to be disturbed. A man who thinks quite differently, you hate him. To live peacefully every day means you have really no nationality, religion, dogma, or authority. Peace means to love, to be kind; if you haven't that, then you are responsible for all the confusion.

9th July 1967

20

2

WE WERE SAYING that it is important to be completely free from the psychological structure of society, that is, to be completely out of society. To understand the problems of the social structure of which we are part and also to be free from them, we need considerable energy, vigor and vitality.

The more one sees how complex society is the more it becomes obvious how complex the individual that lives in society is. The individual is part of the society he has created, his psychological structure is essentially of that society. To understand the problems which each one of us has is to understand the problems of relationship within society—for we have only one problem really and that is the problem of relationship in this social psychological structure. To understand and to be free of the problem of relationship one needs a great deal of energy, not only physical and intellectual energy, but an energy that is not motivated or dependent on any psychological stimulation or on any drugs; to have this energy one must first understand how one dissipates energy. We shall go into it step by step and please realize that the speaker is only a mirror, he is voicing what he hopes is the problem of each one of us; in this way one is not just hearing a series of words and ideas but actually listening to and observing oneself, not in terms of what the speaker or another formulates, but rather one is observing the actual state of one's own confusion, one's own lack of energy, misery, the sense of utter hopelessness and so on.

If one is dependent on any stimulation for the energy which one needs, then that very stimulation makes the mind dull, insensitive, not acute. One may take the drug LSD or other forms of drugs and one may temporarily find enough energy to see things very clearly, but one reverts to one's former state and becomes dependent on that drug more and more. All stimulation, whether of the church, of the drink or drug, or the speaker, will inevitably bring about a dependence and that dependence prevents one from having the vital energy to see clearly for oneself. Any form of dependence on any stimulation lessens the quickness and vitality of the mind. We all depend, unfortunately, on something, it may be dependence on a relationship, or on the reading of an intellectual book, or on certain ideas and ideologies we have formulated; or we depend on solitude, isolation, denial, resistance—these obviously distort and dissipate energy.

One has to become aware of what it is that one is dependent upon. One has to find out why one depends on anything at all, psychologically—I don't mean technologically, or depending on the milkman—but psychologically, why do we depend, what is involved in dependence? This question is essential in investigating the dissipation, deterioration and distortion of energy—the energy we need so vitally to understand the many problems.

What is it on which we so depend, is it a person, a book, a church, a priest, an ideology, a drink or a drug—what are the various supports which each one of us has, subtly or very obviously? Why do we depend and does discovering the cause of a dependence free the mind from that dependence? Do you understand the question? We are taking the journey together—you are not waiting for me to tell you the causes of your dependency, but rather, in enquiring together, we will both discover them—that discovery will be yours, and being yours it will give you vitality. One discovers for oneself that one depends upon something, upon, say, an audience which will stimulate one, therefore one needs that audience. One may derive, from addressing a large group of people, a kind of energy, one depends upon that audience for that energy, upon whether it agrees or disagrees. The more it disagrees the more there is a battle and the more vitality one has, but if the audience agrees then one does not derive that energy. One depends—why? And one asks oneself if in the discovering the cause of one's dependence one will free oneself of that dependence. Go into it slowly with me please. One discovers that one needs an audience because it is a very stimulating thing to address people—why does one need that stimulus? Because in oneself one is shallow, in oneself one has nothing, no source of energy which is always full, rich, vital, which is moving, living. In oneself one is enormously poor, one has discovered that, the cause of one's dependence.

Does the discovery of the cause free one from being dependent or is the discovery of the cause merely intellectual, merely the discovery of a formula? If it is an intellectual investigation and the intellect has found the cause of the mind's dependence, through rationalization, through analysis, then does that free the mind from being dependent? Obviously it doesn't. The mere intellectual discovery of the cause does not free the mind from its dependence on something which will give it stimulation, no more than a merely intellectual acceptance of an idea, or an emotional acquiescence in an ideology will.

The mind is freed from dependence in seeing the totality of this whole structure of stimulation and dependence and in seeing that the mere intellectual discovery of the cause of dependence does not free the mind from dependence. Seeing the whole structure and nature of stimulation and dependence and how that dependence makes the mind stupid, dull, inactive, the seeing of the totality of it, alone, frees the mind.

Does one see the whole picture or does one see only a part of the picture, a detail? This is a very important question to ask oneself, because one sees things in fragments and thinks in fragments—all one's thinking is in fragments. So one must enquire into what it means to see totally. One asks if one's mind can see the whole, even though it has always functioned fragmentarily, as a nationalist, as an individualist, as the collective, as the Catholic, as German, Russian, French, or as an individual caught in a technological society, functioning in a specialized activity, and so on—everything broken up into fragments with good opposed to evil, hate and love, anxiety and freedom. One's mind is always thinking in duality, in comparison, in competition and such a mind functioning in fragments cannot see the whole. If one is a Hindu, if one looks at the world from one's little window as the Hindu, believing in certain dogmas, rituals, traditions, brought up in a certain culture and so on, obviously one does not see the whole of mankind.

So to see something totally, whether it is a tree, or a relationship or any activity that one has, the mind must be free from all fragmentation, and the very nature of fragmentation is the center from which one is looking. The background, the culture as the Catholic, as the Protestant, as the Communist, as the Socialist, as my family, is the center from which one is looking. So as long as one is looking at life from a particular point of view, or from a particular experience which one has cherished, which is one's background, which is the "me," one cannot see the totality. Thus it is not a question of how one is to get rid of fragmentation. One's invariable question would be "how am I who functions in fragments, not to function in fragments?" —but that is a wrong question. One sees that one is dependent psychologically on so many things and one has discovered intellectually, verbally, and through analysis, the cause of that dependence; the discovery is itself fragmentary because it is an intellectual, verbal analytical process—which means that whatever thought investigates must inevitably be fragmentary. One can see the totality of something only when thought doesn't interfere, then one sees not verbally and not intellectually but factually, as I see the fact of this microphone, without any like or dislike, there it is. Then one sees the actuality, that one is dependent and one does not want to get rid of that dependence or to be free of its cause. One observes and one observes without any center, without any structure of the nature of thinking. When there is observation of that kind one sees the whole picture, not just a fragment of that picture and when the mind sees the whole picture there is freedom.

Two things have been discovered, firstly there is a dissipation of energy when there is fragmentation. By observing, by listening to this whole structure of dependence one has discovered that any activity of a mind that works and functions in fragments—as a Hindu, a Communist or a Catholic, or as the analyzer analyzing—is essentially a dissipated mind, a mind that wastes energy. Secondly, that discovery gives one energy to face any fragments that may arise and therefore as one observes those fragments arise there is a resolving of them.

One has found the very source of dissipation of energy, that any fragmentation, any division, any conflict—for division means conflict—is waste of energy. Yet one may think there is no waste of energy if one imitates and accepts authority—depending on the priest, on rituals, on dogma, on the party, on an ideology—because there one accepts and follows. But the following and the acceptance of an ideology, whether it is good or bad, whether it is holy or unholy, is a fragmentary activity and it therefore causes conflict. Conflict will inevitably arise for there will be a division between "what is" and "what should be" and that conflict is a dissipation of energy. Can one see the truth of it? Again it is not "how am I to be free of conflict?" If one puts that question to oneself "how am I to be free of conflict?" then one creates another problem and hence increases conflict. Whereas if one sees,—"sees" as one sees

25

the microphone, clearly, directly,—then one would understand the essential truth of a life in which there is no
conflict at all.

Look Sirs, let us put it differently. We are always comparing what we are with what we should be. The "should
be" is a projection of what we think ought to be. We
compare ourselves with our neighbor, with the riches he has
which we haven't. We compare ourselves with those who
are more bright, more intellectual, more affectionate, more
kind, more famous, more this and that. The "more" plays
an extraordinarily important part of our lives, and the
measuring that takes place in each one of us; measuring
ourselves with something is one of the primary causes of
conflict. In this is involved competition, comparison with
this and with that, and we are caught in this conflict. Now,
why is there comparison at all? Put this question to yourself. Why do you compare yourself with another? Of course
one of the tricks of commercial propaganda is to make you
think you are not what you should be and all the rest of it.
And from a very young age it begins, you must be as clever
as another, through examinations and so on. Why do we
compare ourselves at all, psychologically? Please find out. If
I don't compare, *what am I?* I should be dull, empty,
stupid, I'll be what I am. If I don't compare myself with
another I shall be what I am. But through comparison I
hope to evolve, grow, become more intelligent, more beautiful, more this and more that. Will I? The fact is that I
am what I am and by comparing I am fragmenting that
fact, the actuality, and that is a waste of energy; whereas
not to compare, but to be what actually I am, is to have
the tremendous energy to look. When you can look without comparison you're beyond all comparison—which
doesn't imply a mind that is stagnant with contentment—
on the contrary.

So, we see, in essence, how the mind wastes energy and
how that energy is necessary to understand the totality of
life, not just the fragments. It's like a vast field in which
there are many flowers. Did you not notice, if you were
here earlier, how, before they cut the hay, there were

thousands of flowers of many colors? But most of us take one particular corner of a field and look in that corner at one flower—we don't look at the whole field. We give importance to one flower, and giving importance to that one flower we deny the rest. That's what we do when we give importance to our image of ourselves, then we deny all other images and are therefore in conflict with every other image.

So, as we said, energy is necessary, energy that is without a motive, without a direction. For this we must be poor inwardly, not rich with the things which society, which we have built up. As most of us are rich with the things of society there is no poverty in us at all. What society has built in us and what we have built in ourselves is greed, envy, anger, hate, jealousy, anxiety, and with that we are very rich. To understand all this we must have an extraordinary vitality, both physical as well as psychological. Poverty is one of those strange things; the various religions throughout the world have preached poverty—poverty, chasity, and so on. The poverty of the monk who assumes a robe, changes his name, enters into a cell, picks up the Bible, reads that everlastingly—he's said to be poor. The same is done in different ways in the East, and that's considered poverty—the vow of poverty, to have one loincloth, one robe, one meal a day—and we all respect such poverty. But those people who have assumed the robe of poverty are still rich with the things of society, inwardly, psychologically, because they are still seeking position, prestige; they belong to the category of the religious type and that type is one of the divisions of the culture of society. That is not poverty—poverty is to be completely free of society, though you may have a few clothes, have a few meals. Poverty becomes a marvelous and beautiful thing when the mind is free from the psychological structure of society for then there is no conflict, there is no seeking, there's no asking, no desire—there is nothing. It is only this inward poverty that can see the truth of a life in which there is no conflict at all. Such a life is a benedic-

27

tion, that benediction is not to be found in any church, in any temple.

Questioner: *Is there not a paradox when you say that thought functions always in fragments and to realize that thought functions in fragments needs energy? Is that not a vicious circle?*

KRISHNAMURTI: I need energy to look, but to look becomes fragmentary and therefore dissipates energy—therefore, what is one to do? You see, Sir, I need physical energy, I need intellectual energy, I need an emotional, a passionate energy, to tackle anything—a sustained energy. But I know I am wasting that energy in fragmentation—all the time I'm doing it. Then I say:—"what am I to do, here I am, I want to have this energy to tackle all the problems of life, immediately, but I'm wasting energy all the time"—by not eating the right food, by thinking about this and that, being a Hindu, having my prejudices, my ambitions, envy, greed, and all the rest of it. Now, in that state can I do anything? Listen to the question first, very carefully, don't deny or accept. I dissipate energy and I need energy—that is to say, I'm in a state of contradiction and that very contradiction is another waste of energy. So I realize that whatever I do in this state is a waste of energy. A mind that is confused, whatever it does at any level, will continue to be confused. It is not as if by living according to "one moment of clarity," that confusion will be dissipated. If I do that, then that again breeds another conflict, it therefore furthers more confusion.

I see that any action born of confusion brings, or leads to, further confusion; I've understood that any action of a confused mind only leads to further confusion. I see that very clearly, I see that as a most dangerous thing—as one sees a great danger—I see that as clearly as that. So, what happens? I don't act in terms of confusion anymore. That total inaction is complete action.

Let's put the matter differently. I see that war in any form, killing another from an aeroplane at a great height

28

or with a gun at close quarters, or a battle between my wife and myself, or a battle in business, or a conflict within myself, is war. I may not actually kill a Vietnamese or an American but as long as my life is a battlefield I'm contributing to war. I see that. I see it first, as most of us are trained to, intellectually, that is, fragmentarily, and I see that if I take any action in that fragmentary state it will only contribute to further war, to further conflict. So I must find a state in which there is no conflict at all—a quality of mind that is not touched by conflict. I must find out first of all, if there is such a state, for it may be a purely theoretical, ideological or an imaginary state which is of no value at all. But I have to find it and to find it I must not accept that there is such a state. So, is there such a state? I can only find out if I understand the nature of conflict *totally*—the conflict which is the duality, good and bad—not that there is not the good and not that there is not the bad—and the conflict between love and jealousy. I must look at it without any judgment, without any comparison—just look. I begin to learn how to look, not how to do. I learn how to look at this vast complex field of life, neither accepting nor rejecting, comparing, condemning, justifying—but how to look—as I would look at a tree. I can only really look at a tree when there is no observer, that is, when the fragmentary process of thought doesn't come into being. So I look at this vast battlefield of life which I have taken for granted as the natural way of living, in which I must fight my neighbor, I must fight my wife, I must fight—you know—compare, judge, condemn, threaten, hate. I look at this situation that I've accepted—at this life which is *me*—and then can I really look at myself as I am, without any comparison, condemnation and judgment? When I can, I am already out of society, because society always thinks in terms of the great and the small, the powerful and the weak, the beautiful and the ugly—all the rest of it. With one act I've understood this whole process of fragmentation, and therefore I do not belong to any church, any group, any religion, any nationality, to any party.

Questioner: Reactions of feelings are affected by what you think, and when a mild feeling arises it doesn't affect relationship and you look at it and as long as you don't take any action about it it does seem to fade away, but then a strong antagonistic emotion arises that does affect relationship and you also look at that without taking any action, it doesn't seem to fade away, it continues.

KRISHNAMURTI: To react is perfectly natural, isn't it? If you put a pin into me I will react, unless I'm paralyzed or dead. To react to pleasure and to pain is natural—they are the only two things I have, to react to. The pleasure I want to continue, the pain I want to discard. Reaction is inevitable, natural, but why should it always be broken up into pleasure and pain? I react and then—what takes place? —thought comes in.

Questioner: Before that, if you react violently,—

KRISHNAMURTI: Wait Sir, just look, I react violently—you put a pin into me and I act violently—I hit you back or run away from you which is violence—both are violent. I feel antagonistic later, a second later, when thought comes in and says, I must do something. Observe it Sir, very closely, and you will see it for yourself. You put a pin into me, I react, why should there by any antagonism?

Questioner: Because you're interfering with me.

KRISHNAMURTI: Life is interfering with each one of us all the time.

Questioner: So you resist that.

KRISHNAMURTI: Now find out Sir, why do you resist? Go into it.

Questioner: It's the nature of myself.
30

KRISHNAMURTI: Which is to protect myself physically. I must protect myself physically. Now, why do we carry that desire for protection to psychological states?

Questioner: *Because I don't want to be pushed around psychologically. I want to be free, I don't want to be hemmed in.*

KRISHNAMURTI: Are you?

Questioner: *I am of course, I resist it.*

KRISHNAMURTI: No Sir, you're not following, it's not very clear. Physically there must be protection, because otherwise I couldn't live. Now why does the mind carry over this desire to protect, psychologically. Why?

Questioner: *Because of the self-protective reaction. Mind you, it shouldn't be like that.*

KRISHNAMURTI: No, no, no—don't say "should" or "should not." The fact is, that psychologically we want to protect ourselves, defend ourselves, resist—why?

Questioner: *When it arises it's a fact and when you look at that fact—*

KRISHNAMURTI: Before you go into the fact Sir, find out why you want to protect yourself psychologically.

Questioner: *It's inherent.*

KRISHNAMURTI: There is nothing inherent. Go into it Sir, you will see. Why do I want to protect myself psychologically?

Questioner: *Because my "I" has certain characteristics and that's one of the characteristics. So therefore you want to say that I have to get rid of the "I". But you can't do that.*

31

KRISHNAMURTI: I'm not talking about getting rid of any-thing. Why do I want to protect myself psychologically? I want to protect myself psychologically only when I don't know myself. The more I know myself the less I want to protect—because myself is *nothing*; it's a bundle of words and memories. I am protecting a thing which is not, which is merely an idea, a concept—and I'm protecting *that*, I'm resisting, I'm defending, I'm quarrelling with everybody to maintain it. But the more, or rather, the moment I know the whole structure of that thing, there is nothing to protect. It's not a question of agreeing with me, Sir, do it.

Questioner: Therefore these strong reactions are going to continue until one sees oneself.

KRISHNAMURTI: And if you like to continue with them, you will.

Questioner: Oh yes, but if you don't like them then you have to resist them. That's not right.

KRISHNAMURTI: Look—resistance, defenses, attack, all these are forms of maintaining a certain quality which we think is important, a certain state which we want to protect.

Questioner: It's only part of it.

KRISHNAMURTI: That's a great part of it.

Questioner: There's a question of relationship.

KRISHNAMURTI: All right—put it your own way—relation-ship.

Questioner: Now you don't want to behave in such a way that you have harsh relationships, even though you have the harsh feeling. So there you have to step in and inter-fere.

KRISHNAMURTI: First of all we have to understand what relationship is, before we protect relationship. What is our relationship? If I'm married, if I have a husband, wife, children, what is my relationship with another? Not theoretically—actually—what is my actual relationship with my wife or husband? Have I any relationship at all?

Questioner: You certainly live together.

KRISHNAMURTI: Of course, I live with my wife.

Questioner: And sometimes your relationship is friendly and—

KRISHNAMURTI: Follow it, follow it Sir, go into it. I live with my wife, all the sexual appetites which I had when young have gone, more or less—I still have them occasionally—and what takes place? During the period in which I have lived with my wife I have built up a form of resistance, of dominance, or of acquiescence—I don't want to be nagged, I don't want to be bullied—all that goes on. I have built an image about her in myself and she has built an image about me. Now these two images have a relationship—*not I with her*. So there is no direct relationship—I see this taking place, all my life it has gone on, the image building and the defending of that image, and I see that as long as I have that image about her there must be a contradiction, though I may have a relationship with her as a wife, there is a battle going on, and if I want to live without battle I must first be free of all images. Now, is that possible?—never to create for an instant an image about her. Whatever she does, bullies me, quarrels with me, nags me, whatever it is, never to build an image—is that at all possible? It means that I must have a mind that is so sharp, a mind that is so very alert, that whatever she says never takes root. If you cannot do it, of course you have the relationship of images which will be everlastingly in battle with each other.

Questioner: We're not attacking the same point—because in the office or with people with whom you are associated something may happen and you react with a violent feeling. Well now, the fact is that you're not so alert, that feeling—

KRISHNAMURTI: So, find out why you're not so alert.

Questioner: But in the meantime—

KRISHNAMURTI: There is no meantime.

Questioner: I don't want to quarrel with my office—

KRISHNAMURTI: Well don't quarrel with your office.

Questioner: That's what I mean, then you have to stop that.

KRISHNAMURTI: Stop it. But much more important is, why aren't you alert, aware? If you can answer that then the rest of the questions will be answered. But you want the peripheral questions answered without dealing with the fundamental issue, which is to be aware, to watch yourself.

Questioner (2): How do we know that there is an outside world, how do we know that there's the essence of what the outside world is? Perhaps the outside world is a maya.

KRISHNAMURTI: Now, I believe, the word 'maya' in Sanskrit means 'to measure'. As long as the mind has the capacity to measure it will create illusion—naturally. So they have said that as the mind has no other capacity except to measure, therefore what it measures is illusory. That's a philosophy that exists in India—that all the world is maya, is an illusion. So they say put up with it, forget it, your disease, your hurts, the world, the quarrels—it's just an illusion. But really to tell a hungry man the world is a maya, illusion, means nothing at all to him. A person who has got cancer, pain—to talk to him about illusion means absolutely nothing. What matters is not whether the world exists or doesn't exist, whether it be illusory or not, but the fact is there is the world—there's you and me in battle with each other—Vietnamese are being killed by this or by that. Those are facts and to understand facts we must be in contact with them, which means to look at them without any interference of thought, as prejudice, dogma, belief, nationality.

11th July 1967

3

WE WERE SAYING, the other day, how important it is to understand the nature of conflict, not only outwardly as war, but also inwardly, which is much more complex, needing greater attention and deeper, wider understanding. Most of us are in conflict, at different levels of our consciousness. There is no one spot untouched by conflict. There is no one area which hasn't been a battlefield, and in all our relationships whether with the most intimate person, or with the neighbor, or with society, this conflict exists—a state of contradiction, division, separation, duality, the opposites, all of which contribute to conflict. The more one is aware and just observing oneself and one's relationship to society and its structure, the more we see that at all levels of our being there is conflict—major or minor conflict—which brings about devastating results, or very superficial responses. But the actual fact is, that there is deeply rooted in all of us the essence of conflict, which expresses itself in so many different ways, through antagonism, through hate, through the desire to dominate, to possess, to guide another's life. Now is it at all possible to be totally free of this essence of conflict? Perhaps one can trim, lop off, certain branches of conflict but can one go deeply and unearth the essence so that there is no conflict whatever within and therefore no conflict without? Which does not mean that by becoming free of conflict we shall stagnate, or vegetate, or become undynamic, not vital, not full of energy.

In enquiring about this matter one must first see whether any outward organization can help in bringing about peace within. There are whole groups of people, called by different names, who believe in creating perfect outward organizations—a welfare society bureaucratically run, or a society based on computer thinking, and so on—they believe that such organizations can bring peace to man. There are the Communists, the Materialists, Socialists, and also the so-called religious people who belong to various organizations; they all fundamentally believe that by bringing about a certain order outwardly there will be established through various forms of sanctions, compulsions and laws, freedom from all aggression and from all conflict. Also there is a group of people who say we will have order without conflict, if inwardly we have identified ourselves with a certain principle or ideology and live according to that—according to certain inward, established laws. We know these various types, but through conformity, whether enforced or willing, can there be the cessation of conflict? Do you understand the question? Can there be the cessation of conflict if you are either compelled outwardly to live at peace with yourself and your neighbor—compelled, brainwashed, forced—or, you are inwardly trying to live according to ideologies and principles given to man by authority—forcing yourself, struggling, trying constantly to conform? Man has tried every way—obedience, revolt, conformity and the following of certain directives, in order to live inwardly at peace—without any conflict.

If one observes various civilizations and religions one cannot doubt that man has tried, but somehow, it seems to me, he has always failed. Maybe an altogether different

37

approach is necessary, which is neither conformity, nor obedience, nor imitation nor an identification with a principle, or image, or formula, but a totally different way. By "way" I do not mean a method or a path, but a totally different approach to the whole problem. I think it would be worthwhile examining this possibility together—to find out if it is at all possible for man to live a completely orderly inward life, without any form of compulsion, imitation, suppression, or sublimation and bring it about as a living quality, not something held within the framework of ideas. A peace, an inward tranquillity which knows no disturbance at any moment—is such a state at all possible? I think every intelligent, enquiring human being is asking this question.

Man has accepted war as a way of life; man has accepted conflict as innate, as part of daily existence; man has accepted hate, jealousy, envy, greed, aggression, causing enmity in another, as the natural way of existence. When we accept such a way of life, we must naturally accept the structure of society as it is. If one accepts competition, anger, hate, greed, envy, acquisitiveness, then naturally one lives within the pattern of respectable society. That is what most of us are caught in, because most of us want to be terribly respectable.

Please realize, as we were saying the other day, that merely listening to a few words, or accepting a few ideas, will not solve the problem at all. What we are trying to do together is to examine our own minds, our own hearts, the way we think, the way we feel and how we act in our daily life—to examine what we actually are, not what we should be, or have been. So, if you are listening, then you are listening to yourself, not to the speaker. You are observing the pattern of your own thinking, the way you act, think, feel, live. And there one observes that as long as one conforms to the pattern of society one must accept aggression, hate, enmity, envy, as part of life, that part of life which inevitably breeds conflict, wars, brutality, the so-called modern society. One has to accept it and live with it and in it, making one's life a battlefield. If one does not

38

accept, and no religious person can possibly accept such a society, then how is this inward order with no outward domination to be found?—an inward tranquillity which demands no expression at all, a tranquillity which is in itself a blessing. Is it at all possible to come upon it, and live with it? This is the question which most of us are asking and to which we never find an answer. Perhaps this morning we can go into this question and find out for ourselves whether it is actually possible—not as an idea, not as a concept, but actually find out how to live a daily life in which there is no disorder inwardly, a life of complete tranquillity, but which has tremendous vitality. I think if we could find that out then perhaps all these meetings would be worth-while, otherwise they have no meaning whatever. So let us go into it.

I am tempted to repeat a story about a great disciple going to God and demanding to be taught truth. And this poor God says, "My friend, it is such a hot day, please give me a glass of water." So the disciple goes out, comes upon the first house and knocks on the door, and a beautiful young lady opens the door. The disciple falls in love with her, marries her, and has children—four or five of them. One day, it begins to rain, and it keeps on raining, raining, raining—the torrents have swollen the rivers, the streets are full, houses are being washed away, so the disciple takes his children and his wife, carries them on his shoulder, and as he is being washed away he says, "Lord, please save me!" And the Lord says, "Where is that glass of water for which I asked?" It is rather a good story, because most of us think in terms of time, we think that inward order can only come about through time, that tranquillity is to be built little by little, adding every day. Time does not bring this inward order and peace, so one of the important things to understand is how to put a stop to time so as not to think in terms of gradualness,—which is quite an immense task, which actually means there is no tomorrow for you to be peaceful. You have to be orderly on the instant, there is no other moment.

So we are going to examine the whole structure and

nature of conflict; we are going to do it together, not the speaker alone and you merely a listener, a follower—but rather both of us together, a situation in which there is no authority whatsoever. Because where there is authority, inwardly there is disorder. And since we are investigating together, discovering, understanding, you have to work as hard as the speaker—it is your responsibility, not the speaker's alone.

We know there is inward disorder, inward conflict, which expresses itself outwardly as war, and so on. Being aware of this disorder, this conflict, confusion, and misery, one begins to look, to find out why there is this disorder. Why do we have to live in disorder? Why do we have to have conflict every day—from the moment we wake up till we go to sleep or ultimately die? When we ask such a question, either we answer that it is inevitable and therefore cannot be altered, or we say we don't know the answer, and therefore wait for another to tell us how to look. If we wait for somebody to tell us how to look at this disorder, at this chaos, confusion, conflict, then we are waiting to discover the nature of conflict according to somebody else, therefore we have not discovered. Isn't that so? So it matters immensely how we look, how we say, "why do I live in conflict?" Because when we are no longer seeking any authority to tell us, the moment we are free from the authority of another, we are already clear, our mind is already sharp to look. And to travel, to go up a mountain, we must not carry great burdens. In the same way, if to examine very clearly this complex problem we put away all authority, then we are much lighter, freer to look. Therefore, in order to observe, to act, to listen, there must be freedom from all authority; then we can begin to ask why we live in this dreadful, destructive inward conflict.

I wonder, when you look, what is your response? Is it to the causes of conflict, or to the person with whom you are in conflict, or to the division between what you want and its contrary—or is it to the very nature of conflict? I don't want to know with whom I am in conflict, I don't want to know the peripheral conflicts of my being. What I want to know, in essence, is why should conflict exist at all? When I put that question to myself, I see a fundamental issue, which has nothing to do with peripheral conflicts and their solution. I am concerned with the central issue, and I see, perhaps you also see, that the very nature of desire, if not properly understood, inevitably leads to conflict.

I desire contradictory things. Desire itself is always in contradiction; which doesn't mean that I must destroy desire—suppress it, control it, sublimate it. I see that desire in itself is contradictory—not the desire for something, for achievement, for success, for prestige, for having a better house, better knowledge, and so on, not in the object, but in the very nature of desire itself, there is contradiction. Now, I have to understand the nature of desire before I can understand conflict and when I am concerned with it I am neither condemning, justifying, nor suppressing it. I am just aware of the nature of desire, in which there is a contradiction, and that this contradiction breeds conflict. We are in ourselves in contradiction, wanting this and not wanting that, wanting to be more beautiful or more intelligent, wanting more power. In ourselves we are in a state of contradiction, and that state of contradiction is brought about by desire—desire for pleasure and the avoidance of pain.

So I see desire as the root of all contradiction. Desire says I must have this, I must avoid that—I must have pleasure, whether sexual, or the pleasure of becoming famous, the pleasure of dominating, pleasures of various subtle kinds. Not achieving these, not being able to arrive at what I want, there is the pain of not achieving, which is a contradiction. So we live in a state of contradiction; I must think this, but I think that; I must be that, but actually I am this; there must be brotherhood of mankind, but I am nationalistic; I cling to my church, my God, my house, my family. So we live in contradiction. That is our life. And that contradiction cannot be integrated; that is one of the fallacies. Contradiction only comes to an end when I begin to understand the whole nature of desire. Throughout the world, in the Orient and the Occident, there are people who are interested in this, the so-called religious people—not the business man, not the army people, not the bureaucrats, they are not interested in any of these things, but the so-called religious people—knowing that desire is the root of all these things, they have said that it must be suppressed, sublimated, destroyed, controlled. But what is happening? Some Catholic priests are in revolt and want to get married and the monk is now looking outward. All the agonies of suppression, distortion, the brutal discipline of conformity to a pattern, have no meaning whatsoever, they don't lead to truth. To understand truth the mind must be completely free, without distortion—not a spot of it.

One has to understand this question of desire, but not intellectually, for there is no such thing as intellectual understanding. When one says, "I understand intellectually," what one actually means is, "I hear the words, and I understand the meaning of the words." So when one uses the word 'understanding', one is saying that to understand is to be immediately aware of the fact. If you are immediately aware of the fact there is understanding which is also action. So one has to find out what desire is. Why shouldn't there be desire and what is wrong with desire? When one sees a beautiful house, a lovely stream, a cloud lit by the evening sun over the mountain, when you look at all that, there is immense sensual pleasure, the enjoyment of lovely color and so on. What is wrong with it? Why should one suppress it? And when one sees a lovely face, why shouldn't one look at that face? We know how desire arises, it is a very simple and a very obvious phenomenon that doesn't need a great deal of investigation. There is seeing, contact, sensation, and when thought interferes with that sensation desire arises. I can look at that beautiful face, well proportioned, intelligent, alive, not self-centered, it is not self-conscious of its own beauty and therefore no longer beautiful; I can look at it and the looking brings a sensation, and then thought comes in and all the things that thought developes, possession, holding, sex—the whole process begins, by thought. So the reaction is perverted by thought.
42

But to react is normal, healthy, sane. It would be absurd to see a marvelous light on the cloud and not enjoy it, but thought dwells upon it and makes it into a pleasurable memory, and it wants that pleasure to be repeated. This is the whole nature of sex, thought chews over the pleasure, over and over again and it wants it to be repeated. So there is thought and desire which are always in contradiction with each other. Is it clear? Look, these are only ordinary explanations and as explanations have no value at all. But what has value is to see how desire comes into being, how thought interferes with sensation and makes it into a memory and the desire for the pleasure of that memory is given continuity and sustained by thought, nourished by thought.

Thought and desire must always be in contradiction in themselves because they are fragmentary. As we said the other day, all thought is fragmentary, and therefore desire is a contradiction. Our life is in a state of self contradiction from morning until night, until we die. And one sees this actually, not theoretically, not verbally, not intellectually, one sees this thing as one sees from a height the whole valley, the beauty of the valley, the stream, the trees, the people, the houses, the color, the whole thing one sees. In the same way one looks at this thing, and one sees that one cannot do anything about it. What can one do? If one does anything, it is the action of thought wanting to change it and therefore bringing another contradiction.

I see in myself a state of contradiction. I see how this contradiction has arisen, and that this contradiction is disorder and that there can be no order brought about by thought, because thought in itself is fragmentary, is limited; thought is the response of memory, and when that memory which is fragmentary, acts upon this contradiction it breeds further contradiction. So I see the whole of this phenomenon and the very *seeing is the action within which there is no contradiction.* Look, let's put it very simply. I see I am dull, stupid—the response to that is, I want to be more clever, intelligent, brighter. Now what has happened? I am dull, stupid, and I want to be brighter, more intelligent, in that there is contradiction already, therefore there is further conflict which is a further waste of energy. But if I could live with that stupidity, with that dullness, without the contradiction and therefore with the capacity to look at that dullness, it would be no longer dull. I don't know if you see? Or, I am envious and I don't want to change it, I don't want to become non-envious—the fact is, I am envious. Can I look at that envy without introducing its opposite, without wanting not be envious, or to change it, or to be specific about it? Can I look at that envy, which is a form of hate and jealousy, can I look at it, as it is, without introducing any other factor? The moment I introduce any other factor I bring in further contradiction. But envy in itself is a contradiction, isn't it? I am this, I want to be that, and so long as there is any form of comparative thinking, there must be conflict. And this does not mean that I am satisfied with what I am, for the moment I am satisfied with what I am I only breed further conflict. Can I look at my envy without bringing about conflict in that look? Can I just look at a beautiful house, a lovely garden with flowers, without any contradiction? Contradiction must exist as long as there is division, and the very nature of desire, which thought builds up, is to bring about division.

So to have inward order, inward tranquility and a mind that is not in conflict at any time, one has to understand the whole nature of thought and desire, and that understanding can only exist when thought doesn't breed further conflict.

Just a minute, Sir, just a minute. Let us take a breather, shall we? You know, it is very odd that you come prepared with questions and therefore you are not listening to the talk. You are more interested in the question that you are going to put than in listening to what has been said. Sir, take time, have a little patience, because we have talked about something very serious that demands a great deal of enquiry, a great deal of looking into. If you have looked

44

deeply into yourselves, you have no time to ask a question so immediately.

Questioner: What is going to prevent a new religion, with a dogma with a church and a priest and an interpreter being formed of what you are saying?

KRISHNAMURTI: I am afraid nobody can prevent it except yourself. Isn't that so? If you are a follower then you destroy everything and you will invent a new sect, a new religion, a new priest, a new dogma and all that filth. And I am using that word filth properly. So it depends on you, whether you are going to use this to exploit it, to achieve a particular position, a particular understanding and all the rest of it. It is so simple.

Questioner: Can this freedom from conflict take place while we are in deep sleep?

KRISHNAMURTI: I don't know anything about deep sleep, but what I want is to be free from this conflict while I am awake, while I go and work in a beastly little office, with my bosses and all the rest of it; in my family there must be peace and order in myself, while I am awake. You know, a sleep in which there is no dreaming at all is one of the most extraordinary things—I don't know if you want to go into it and if this is the right occasion. Shall we go into it? That gentleman raised the question whether this freedom from conflict exists in deep sleep? If in our daily life it doesn't exist, it cannot possibly exist when we are asleep, and this question raises the whole problem of dreams and sleep.

The psychologists, the fashionable ones and the well established ones, say that you must dream otherwise something is wrong with you. We have never asked ourselves why we dream at all. We have never asked ourselves whether we can give the mind complete rest, not only at those moments when we are alone in solitude with ourselves, but also when we are asleep—but to have complete rest, without any dreams, without any conflict, without any problems. In that state the mind can renew itself, can become fresh, young, innocent. But if the mind is all the time tortured by problems, by conflict, by innumerable contradictory desires, then dreams are inevitable. So let's go into it.

Find out for yourselves why you dream at all, not how to interpret dreams. Why do you dream and is it necessary to dream? You dream because during the day your mind is so occupied with outward things, your office, the kitchen, washing dishes, the children, outwardly occupied with the radio, the television, the newspaper, the magazine, the trees, the rivers, the clouds and everything that is imping-ing upon your mind. At those moments there is no hint of the unconscious. Obviously when the surface mind is very occupied, the deeper layers of consciousness, of that mind, have no relationship with it. And when you go to sleep, the superficial mind, which has been so occupied during the day, is somewhat quiet—not entirely quiet, but somewhat quiet. I am not a psychologist, I am not a specialist, but I have observed this and you can do it for yourselves. So when you go to sleep the superficial mind is fairly quiet and then the deeper layers intimate their own demands, their own conflicts, their own agonies. And these become certain forms of dreams, with intimations, hints. Then you wake up and say "By Jove, I have had a dream, it tells me something, or I must do something with it." Or as you are dreaming the interpretation is going on. If you have ever followed a dream, as you are dreaming, the interpretation is also taking place. Then when you wake up your prob-lems are solved, your mind is lighter, fairly clear. Now all that process is a waste of energy, isn't it? Why should you dream at all? Because if you are really awake during the day, watching every thought, every feeling, every movement of the mind, your angers, your bitterness, your envies, your hates, your jealousies, watching your reactions when you are flattered, when you are insulted, when you are neglect-ed, when you feel lonely, watching all that, and the trees, the movement of the water, being greatly aware of everything outside you, inwardly, then the whole of the uncon-sciousness, as well as the conscious, is opened up. You don't have to wait for the night to sleep, to have the intimations of the unconscious. Then, if you do this, watch your mind in operation, your feelings, your heart, your reactions—that is, if you know yourself as you are in your relationships with the outer and with your own feelings—then you will see that when you go to sleep there is no dreaming at all. Then the mind becomes an extraordinary instrument which is always renewing itself—because there is no conflict at all, it is always fresh. And this is not a theory, you can't practice it. Such a mind is, by its very nature, really tranquil, quiet, silent. It is only such a mind that can see the beauty of life; and such a mind alone can know, can come upon, something which is beyond time.

13 July 1967

4

We are very serious about rather trivial things but very few of us are serious and earnest about the fundamental issues of life. We are serious in demanding and fulfilling our desires and pleasures. We are serious in self-expression or in continuing a particular activity to which we are committed. We are serious about nationalism, about wars, about our particular prejudices, dogmas and beliefs. At least we are superficially serious, but unfortunately we are not serious about the deep issues of life. And the more one is serious about the radical implications of life the more one has vigor, vitality, and the drive that is necessary to go through to the very end. It seems to me that here in this tent we should be clear, at least for the time being, clear and serious in what we are talking about.

We were saying how extraordinarily important it is to bring about a psychological revolution so that we are totally outside society. There have been many revolutions, economic, social, ideological, but unfortunately they have brought about colossal misery, and peripheral improvement—they have not in any way solved the human problem of relationship. When we talk about revolution we are concerned with the *psychological* structure of society in which we are caught and of which we are part. And apparently we are not very serious about the psychological structure or the psychological nature of our being which has brought about a society which is so corrupt and which really has very little meaning. We don't take very seriously the question of how to be free from that society. At least there must be a few, a group of people, not organized around a particular form of dogma, belief, or leader, but rather a group of individuals who are seriously and with complete intent, aware of the nature of their psyche and of society and of the necessity of inwardly bringing about a total revolution—that is, no longer living in violence, in hatred, in antagonism, in merely pursuing every form of entertainment and pleasure. Pleasure and desire are not love. We pursue pleasure and desire and their fulfilment, sexually, or ambitiously—which we call love—at different levels of our existence, and this pursuit we consider imperative, necessary and demanding complete attention.

What we are concerned about, in this tent, during these talks and discussions, is to see if as individuals we can bring about in ourselves that quality of seriousness which in itself, through awareness of one's own nature, brings about a revolution: to bring this about, not through propaganda, not because we are here every other day for the next three weeks, not because we conform to a particular ideological pattern, but rather as human beings gathered together to understand the very complex problem of living— not belonging to any group, any society, any nationality, to any particular dogma, religion, church, and all that immature nonsense. So we are trying during these days to bring about in ourselves that quality of seriousness, which in itself, through awarenes of its own nature—never accepting, never condemning, but observing its relationship to society —will bring about a revolution. That is what we are concerned with and with nothing else. Because everything else is rather immature, everything else leads to antagonism, to

49

war, to hatred. Also we are concerned with action, not ideological action, not action according to a particular principle, or action according to Communism, Socialism, Capitalism, or action according to a particular religious dogma or sanction, but the action of a mind which, because it has freed itself from the sociological and psychological structure of society, has become a religious mind.

By "religious mind" we mean a mind that is aware not only of the outward circumstances of life and of how society is built, of the complex problems of outward relationships, but also aware of its own mechanism, of the way it thinks, it feels, it acts. Such a mind is not a fragmentary mind; such a mind is not concerned with the particular, whether the particular is the "me" or society, or a particular culture, or a particular dogma or ideology but rather it is concerned with the total understanding of man, which is ourselves.

What we are inwardly exposes itself outwardly. You may introduce many laws, many injunctions, sanctions and tortures outwardly, but unless there is an inward revolution, inward change, the mere outward structure of what "should be" is ultimately broken down; you may put man in a frame-work so tight, as in the communist world, yet it will break up. So we are in this world that is so confused, so miserable, at war; can we, living in this world, as human beings, bring about a change in ourselves? That seems to me the fundamental issue, not what you believe, or what you don't believe whether you are a Christian, non-Christian, whether you are a Catholic, Protestant and all the immature structures which the mind has built upon fear.

What are we, as human beings, concerned about—what is it that is most important for us, apart from the routine of daily living, going to the office and all that goes with that—what is fundamentally serious to each one of us? I think we should ask that question of ourselves, not to find an easy answer—and when we do put such a question earnestly, deeply, we shall begin then to find out for ourselves, whether money, position, prestige, fame, success, whether these things and all the implications involved in them, are really most important for each one of us. Or, are we pursuing a secret pleasure of our own—that pleasure of having a greater experience, greater knowledge, greater understanding of life, which again is the pursuit of pleasure in different forms? And we may be very serious, seeking to find out what truth is and if there is such a thing as God yet is not that search, is not the pursuit of that, also tinged with pleasure? Or, are we merely pursuing physical satisfaction—sensorily, sexually, and so on? Of these things I think we should be very clear, because they are going to guide and shape our lives. Most of us are pursuing, outwardly and inwardly, pleasure, and pleasure is the structure of society. I think it is very important to find this out, because from childhood till death, deeply, surreptitiously, cunningly and also obviously, we are pursuing pleasure, whether it be in the name of God, in the name of society, or in the name of our own demands and urgencies. And if we are pursuing pleasure, which most of us are, which we can observe very simply, what is implied in that pursuit? I may want pleasure, I may want the fulfilment of that pleasure, through ambition, through hate, through jealousy; and so on—if I know, or observe, for myself, the nature and structure of pleasure then in the understanding of it I can either pursue it logically, ruthlessly, acting with fully open eyes though it involves a great deal of fear and pain—or come upon a state in which I can live in peace.

It is important, it seems to me, that one should understand the nature of pleasure—not condemning it or justifying it, or keeping it in a deep corner of one's mind which one never examines because it may reveal a pleasure that may contain in itself tremendous pain. I think we should investigate closely, honestly, delicately, this question, neither opposing it nor resisting it—for pleasure is a basic demand of our life, the finding of it and the continuity of that pleasure, in nourishing it and sustaining it, and when there is no pleasure, life becomes dull, stupid, lonely, tiresome, meaningless.

Intellectuals throughout the world have found that pleasure doesn't bring a great deal of understanding, and because of this they have invented philosophies, theologies, according to the clever, cunning mind. But those of us who are serious must find out what pleasure is, what is the nature of it, why we are caught in it. We are not condemning pleasure, we are not saying it is right or wrong. People are violent because it gives them a great deal of pleasure—they get a great deal of satisfaction and pleasure from hurting somebody, verbally, physically, or by a gesture. Or one takes pleasure in becoming famous, writing a book. So one must find out what pleasure is and what is involved in it, and whether it is at all possible to live in a world that contains not pleasure but a tremendous sense of bliss, a tremendous sense of enjoyment, which is not pleasure at all. We are going to investigate that this morning—investigate it together, not by the speaker explaining and you listening, agreeing or disagreeing, but rather by taking the journey together. To take the journey together you must travel lightly and you can only travel lightly when you are not burdened with opinions and conclusions.

Why is it that the mind is always demanding pleasure? Why is it that we do things, however noble or ignoble, with the under-current of pleasure? Why is it that we sacrifice, give up, suffer—again on the thin thread of pleasure? And what is pleasure? I wonder if any of us have seriously asked ourselves this question and pursued it to the very end to find out? Obviously it arises from sensory reactions—I like you or I don't like you—you look nice or you don't look nice—that's a lovely cloud, full of light, the beauty and shape of that mountain, clear against the blue sky. Sensory perception is involved and there is a deep delight in watching the flow of a river, watching a face that is well proportioned, intelligent, has depth. And then there is the memory of yesterday which was full of deep enjoyment, whether it was sexual or intellectual, or merely a fleeting emotional response—and one wants yesterday's pleasure repeated—again it is a form of sensory reaction. Yesterday evening one saw a cloud on the top of the mountains, lit by the setting sun; as one observed it there was no "observer" but only the light and the beauty of that sunset—that left an imprint on the mind and the mind thinks it over and demands a further experience of that nature. These are obvious everyday phenomena in our lives, whether the perception of a cloud or a sexual or intellectual experience.

So thought has a great deal to do with pleasure. I can look at that sunset and the next moment it is gone—thought comes in and begins to think about it, says how beautiful it was when for a moment "I" was absent, with all my problems, tortures, miseries; there was only that marvelous thing. And that remains as thought, is sustained by thought. The same thing with regard to sexual pleasure—thought chews it over, thinks about it endlessly, builds up images which sustain the sensation and the demand for fulfilment tomorrow. It is the same with regard to ambition, fame, success and being important. So desire is sustained and nourished by thought, it is given continuity in relation to a particular form of experience which has given pleasure. One can observe this very simply in oneself. And when that thought, which has created pleasure, is denied, then there is pain, there is conflict—then there is fear. Please do observe this in yourself, otherwise there is no value at all in what you are hearing. What you hear, the explanation, is like the noise of a roaring stream, it has no value at all, but if you listen, not to the speaker, but use the speaker as a mirror in which you are looking, then you will relate what is being said to yourself, and it may have tremendous value. I hope that you are doing this, because without understanding pleasure and therefore pain, we shall never be free of fear.

A mind that is not clear of fear lives in darkness, in confusion, in conflict. A mind that is caught in fear must be violent, and the whole psychological structure as well as the sociological life of a human being, is based on the pleasure/fear principle—therefore he is aggressive, violent. You may have ideologies and principles of non-violence, but they are all utterly meaningless. As we said the other day, all ideologies, whether of the communists, of the churches

53

or of a serious person, are idiotic, they have no meaning. What has meaning is to understand fear and to understand fear one must also understand, very deeply, the nature of pleasure. Pleasure involves pain, the two are not separate, they are two sides of a single coin. To understand pleasure one must be fully aware of the subleties of this pleasure. Have you ever noticed how people talk when they have a little power, when they are at the head of some silly, stupid organization?—they thunder like God because they have a little power. That means that to them pleasure has become an extraordinarily important thing. And if they are a little intellectual or famous, how their manner, walk and outlook changes.

So where there is pleasure there is pain inevitably leading to fear—not only fear of great things, like death, like the fear of deep lonely isolation, fear of not being at all, but also at superficial levels, the fear of what a neighbor thinks about you, how the boss at the office regards you, of the husband and wife, and the fear of not living up to images that one has built about oneself. The fear not only of the unknown, but fear of the known. And all this fear is resolved, not by suppression, not by denial, but by understanding the whole structure of pleasure, pain and fear. For that understanding there is required an awareness which comes when you are looking at yourself, looking at yourself as in a mirror—because without self-knowing, that is, knowing about yourself, pleasure and fear can never come to an end.

To know yourself is to know a very complex and living thing—it is like a movement, a constant moving, moving, moving. To know yourself, to observe, you must have a mind in which there is no sense of comparison or judgment or condemnation or justification. After all, life being an immense living movement, it is not to be limited to your idiosyncrasies or fancies, or your demands—although these are also part of that movement—and if you confine that movement to the particular form of your demands and inclinations then you will always remain in conflict.

A mind that has understood the nature of pleasure and

fear is no longer violent and can therefore live at peace within itself and with the world.

Perhaps we can talk over together, through questioning, what we have discussed this morning.

Questioner: How can we have trust in the speaker so that we may know that what he is saying is true? And how can we have trust in him so that we may know that he leads us rightly?

KRISHNAMURTI: Are we talking about leadership and trust? You know we have had leaders of every kind, political, religious. Aren't you fed up with the leaders? Haven't you thrown them overboard into that river so that you have no leader at all any more? Or are you still, after these two million years, seeking a leader? Because leaders destroy the follower and the followers destroy the leader. Why should you have faith in anyone?

The speaker does not demand your faith, he is not setting himself up as an authority, because an authority of any kind—especially in the field of thought, of understanding—is the most destructive, evil thing. So we are not talking of leadership, of having faith in the leader or the speaker. We are saying that each one of us, each one of us as a human being, has to be one's own leader, teacher, disciple, everything in oneself. Everything else has failed, the churches, the political leaders, the leaders of war, those people who want to bring about a marvelous society, they have not done it. So it depends on you now, on you as a human being, in whom the whole of mankind is, it is your responsibility. Therefore you have to become tremendously aware of yourself, of what you say, of how you say it, of what you think and the motives in the pursuit of your pleasures.

Questioner: What is the relationship between pleasure and fear?

55

KRISHNAMURTI: Don't you know it, do you want an explanation of that? When I can't get my pleasure what happens? Have you not noticed it? I want something which is going to give me tremendous pleasure—what takes place when I am thwarted, denied it? There is antagonism, there is violence, there is a sense of frustration, all of which is a form of fear.

So let us examine this question of pleasure and fear. I want something which is going to give me a great deal of pleasure. I want to become famous, have position, prestige —then that is denied—what happens to me? Or when you have denied yourself the pleasure of drinking, of smoking or having sex, or whatever it is—have you noticed what battles you go through, what pain, what anxiety, what antagonism, hatred. It is all a form of fear, isn't it—I'm afraid of not getting what I want? Aren't you afraid, having climbed for many years to a particular form of ideology, when that ideology is shaken, torn away from you by logic or by life, aren't you afraid of standing alone? The belief in that ideology has given you satisfaction and pleasure, and when that is taken away you are left stranded, empty handed, and fear begins—until you find another form of belief, another pleasure. It is so simple and because it is so simple we refuse to see its simplicity, we want it to be very complex. When your wife turns away from you aren't you jealous—aren't you angry—aren't you hating the man who has attracted her? And what is all that but fear of losing that which has given you a great deal of pleasure, a companionship, a certain quality of assurance, and domination and all the rest.

You know it is most difficult to look at things simply, for our minds are very complex—we have lost the quality of simplicity. I don't mean simplicity in clothes, in food, in all that immature nonsense which the saints cultivate, but the simplicity of a mind that can look directly at things— that can without any fear look at oneself as one actually is, without any distortion, so that when you lie, you see you
56

lie—not cover it up, not run away from it, not find excuses. When you are afraid, know you are afraid, be clear about your fear.

16th July 1967

5

WE SAID THAT we were going to talk over together this morning the question of fear. As it is a very important subject we should spend not only this morning, but perhaps several mornings, going into that question and all the problems related to that central issue, which is fear.

Before we begin to unravel the very complex issue of fear we should also, I think, understand the nature of freedom. What do we mean by freedom and do we really want to be free? I am not at all sure that most of us want to be completely free of every burden, rather we should like to keep some pleasurable, satisfying, complex ideologies and gratifying formulas. We should of course like to be free of those things that are painful—the ugly memories, painful experiences and so on. So we should go into this question of freedom and enquire whether it is at all possible to be free, or if it is an ideological utopia, a concept which has no reality whatsoever. We all say we would like to be free, but I think that before we pursue that desire with which our inclinations or tendencies confront us, we should understand the nature and the structure of freedom. Is it freedom when you are free from something, free from pain, free from some kind of anxiety; or is not freedom itself entirely different from freedom from something? One can be free from anger, perhaps from jealousy, but is not freedom from something a reaction and therefore not freedom at all?

Is not freedom something entirely different from any reaction, any inclination, any desire? One can be free from dogma very easily, by analyzing, kicking it out, yet the motive for that freedom from a dogma contains its own reaction, doesn't it? The motive, the desire to be free from a dogma, may be that it is no longer convenient, no longer fashionable, no longer reasonable, no longer popular, circumstances are against it and therefore you want to be free from it; these are merely reactions. Is reaction away from anything freedom—or is freedom something entirely different from reaction, standing by itself without any motive, not dependent upon any inclination, tendency and circumstance? Is there such a thing as that kind of freedom? One can be free from nationalism because one believes in inter-nationalism, or because it is no longer economically necessary with a Common Market in which it is no longer worth keeping the dogma of nationalism with its flag; you can easily put that away. But has such rationalization or logical conclusion anything to do with freedom? Nor can a leader, spiritual or political, promise freedom at the end of something—for can freedom which comes about through discipline, through conformity, through acceptance, that promises the ideal through the following of that ideal, be freedom? Or is freedom a state of mind which is so intensely active, vigorous, that it throws away every form of dependence, slavery, conformity and acceptance? Does the mind want such freedom? Such freedom implies complete solitude, a state of mind which is not dependent on circumstantial stimulation, ideas, experience. Freedom of that kind obviously means aloneness, solitude. Can the mind brought up in a culture that is so dependent upon environment, on its own tendencies, inclinations, ever find that freedom which is completely alone? It is only in such solitude that there can be relationship with another; in it there is no friction, no dominance, no dependence. Please, you have to understand this, it is not just a verbal conclusion, which you accept or deny. Is this what each individual demands and insists upon—a freedom in which there is no leadership, no tradition, no authority? Otherwise there is not freedom; otherwise when you say you are free from something, it is merely a reaction, which, because it is a reaction, is going to be the cause of another reaction. One can have a chain of reactions, accepting each reaction as a freedom, but that chain is not freedom, it is a continuity of the modified past to which the mind clings.

Freedom from fear can be reaction, but such a reaction is not freedom. I can be free from the fear of my wife, but I may still be afraid. I may be free from the fear of my wife but freedom from that form of fear is particular —I don't like to be dominated and therefore I want to be free from domination, from the nagging and all the rest. That particular demand for freedom is a reaction which will create another form of conformity, another form of domination. Like the beatniks, the hippies and so on, their revolt against society, which is good in itself, is a reaction which is going to create a conformity to the hippies, therefore it is not freedom at all.

When we discuss the question of fear, we must, of necessity, understand the nature of freedom, or see that when we talk about freedom we are not talking about complete freedom, but rather freedom from some inconvenient, unpleasant, undesirable thing. We don't want to be free from pleasure; we want to be free from pain. But pain is the shadow of pleasure—the two cannot be separated, they are the one coin with pleasure and pain on reverse sides.

Freedom is complete in itself, it is not a reaction, it is not an ideological conclusion. Freedom implies complete solitude, an inward state of mind that is not dependent on any stimulus, on any knowledge; it is not the result of any experience or conclusion. In understanding freedom we also understand what is implied in solitude. Most of us, inwardly, are never alone. There is a difference between isolation, cutting oneself off and aloneness, solitude. We know what it is to be isolated, to have built a wall around oneself, a wall of resistance, a wall which we have built in order never to be vulnerable. Or we may live in a dreamy, idiotic ideology which has no validity at all. All these bring about self-isolation, and in our daily life, in the office, at home, in our sexual relationships, in every activity, this process of self-isolation is going on. That form of isolation, and living in an ivory tower of ideology, has nothing whatsoever to do with solitude, with aloneness. The state of solitude, aloneness, can only come about when there is freedom from the psychological structure of society, which we have built through our reactions and of which we are.

In understanding total freedom we come upon the sense of complete solitude. I feel that it is only a mind that has understood this solitude that can have relationship in which there is no conflict whatsoever. But if we create an image of what we think is solitude and establish that as the basis of solitude in ourselves, and from that try to find a relationship, then such relationship will only bring about conflict.

We are concerned with the question of fear, but if we don't understand the problems related to that central issue, that quality of aloneness, then when we approach that thing called fear we shan't know what to do. We were saying, that we human beings—who have lived so long, gathered so much experience—are second-hand entities, there is nothing original. We are contaminated by every kind of torture, conflict, obedience, acceptance, fear, jealousy, anxiety and therefore there is not that quality of aloneness. Please observe yourself—as we said the other day, do use the speaker and his words as a mirror in which you are observing yourself. The more you know about yourself the greater the quality of maturity—the immature person is he who does not know himself at all. One of the main features of fear is the non-acceptance of what one is, the inability to face oneself.

We as human beings, as we are, are only a result, a psychological product. In that state—in being a product of time, of culture, of experience, of knowledge, of all the accumulated memories of a thousand yesterdays, or of yesterday—there is no aloneness at all. All our relationships are based on what has been, or what should be, therefore all relationship is a conflict, a battlefield. If one would understand what is right relationship, one must enquire into the nature and the structure of solitude, which is to be completely alone. But that word *alone* creates an image—watch yourself, you will see. When you use that word *alone* you have already a formula, an image, and you try to live up to that image, to that formula. But the word or the image is not the fact. One has to understand and live with that which actually is. We are not alone, we are a bundle of memories, handed down through centuries, as Germans, as Russians, as Europeans, and so on.

Understanding solitude—if you really know what it means and live in that state—is really quite extraordinary, because then the mind is always fresh and is not dependent upon inclination, tendency, not guided by circumstance. In understanding solitude you will begin to understand the necessity of living with yourself as you actually are—for one of our major causes of fear is that we do not want to face ourselves as we are. Please, this morning, do look at yourselves as you actually are, not as you think you ought to be or as you have been. See whether you can look at yourself without any tremor, without any false modesty, without any fear, without any justification or condemnation—just live with what you actually are.

Know what it means to live with actuality. In observing myself I find I am jealous, anxious, or envious—I realize that. Now I want to live with that because it is only when I live with something intimately that I begin to understand it. But to live with my envy, with my anxiety, is one of the most difficult things—I see that the moment I get used to it I am not living with it. You are following all this? There is that river and I can see it every day, hear the sound of it, the lapping of the water, but after two or three days I have got used to it and I don't always hear it. I can have a picture in the room, I have looked at it every day, at the beauty, the color, the various depths and shadows, the quality of it, yet having looked at it for a week I have lost it, I have got used to it. And the same happens with the mountains, with the valleys, the rivers, the trees, with the family, with my wife, with my husband. But to live with a living thing like jealousy, envy, means that I can never accept it, I can never get used to it—I must care for it as I would care for a newly planted tree, I must protect it against the sun, against the storm. So, in the same way, I have to live with this anxiety and envy, I must care for it, not get used to it, not condemn it. In this way I begin to love it and to care for it, which is not that I love to be envious or anxious, but rather that I care for the watching. It is like living with a snake in the room, gradually I begin to see my immediate relationship to it and there is no conflict.

So, can you and I, live with what we actually are? Being dull, envious, fearful, thinking that we have tremendous affection when we have not, getting easily hurt, flattered, bored, can we live with these actualities, neither accepting nor denying, but observing, living with them without becoming morbid, depressed or elated? Then you will find that one of the major reasons for fear is that we don't want to live with what we are.

We have talked, first of freedom, then of solitude and then of being aware of what we are, and also of how what we are is related to the past and has a movement towards the future, of being aware of this and of living with it, never getting used to it, never accepting it. If we understand this, not intellectually, but through actually doing it, then we can ask a further question: is this freedom, this solitude, this actual coming into immediate contact with the whole structure of what is, to be found or to be come upon through time? That is, is freedom to be achieved through time, through a gradual process? I am not free, because I am anxious, I am fearful, I am this, I am that, I am afraid of death, I am afraid of my neighbor, I am afraid of losing my job, I am afraid of my husband turning against me—of all the things that one has built up through life. I am not free. I can be free by getting rid of them one by one, throwing them out, but that is not freedom. Is freedom to be achieved through time? Obviously not—for the moment you introduce time there is a process, you are enslaving yourself more and more. If I am to be free from violence gradually, through the practice of non-violence, then in the gradual practice I am sowing the seeds of violence all the time. So we are asking a very fundamental question when we ask whether freedom is to be achieved, or rather, whether it comes into being, through time?

The next question is—can one be conscious of that freedom? You are following? If one says "I am free," then one is not free. So freedom, the freedom of which we are talking, is not something resulting from a conscious effort to achieve it. Therefore it lies beyond all, beyond the field of consciousness and it is not a matter of time. Time is consciousness; time is sorrow; time is fear of thought. When you say, "I have realized that complete freedom," then you certainly know, if you are really honest with yourself, that you are back where you were. It is like a man saying "I am happy," the moment he says "I am happy," he is living the memory of that which is gone. Freedom is not of time and the mind has to look at life, which is a vast movement, without the bondage of time. Do go into it, you will see that one can do all this and when this is very clear—not ideologically, not because you have accepted explanations—then one can proceed to find out what fear is and whether it is at all possible to be completely free of it, right through one's being.

One may be superficially aware or conscious of fear. I may be afraid of my neighbor and know I am afraid; I can resist, or neglect, or be totally indifferent to what he says because I think he is stupid—I can resist him. I can be aware of my conscious fears, but am I aware of my fears at the deeper levels of my mind? How are you going to find out the fears that are concealed, hidden, secret? This implies a much graver question, which is—is fear to be divided into the conscious and the unconscious? Please follow this closely, it is a very important question. The specialist, the psychologist, the analyst, has made this division into the deeper levels of fear and the superficial levels of fear. But if you follow what the psychologists say, or what the speaker says, then you are understanding their theory, their dogmas, their knowledge—you are understanding the actuality of yourself. You can't understand yourself according to Freud, Jung or according to the speaker—you have to understand yourself directly. For this reason all those people have no importance at all.

We are asking—is fear to be divided, as the conscious fears and the unconscious fears? Please be careful how you answer this question, for if you say they are not to be divided then you are denying the unconscious. If you accept that fears are to be divided into the conscious and the unconscious, then you accept that formula. See what is implied when you make the division into fears of the deeply rooted unconscious and the superficial fears. What is implied in that? One can be fairly easily conscious and aware and know the superficial fears by one's immediate reactions. But to unearth, unravel, uproot, to expose the deep-rooted fears, how is that to take place—through dreams, through intimations, through hints? All that implies time. Or is there only fear, which fear we translate into different forms? Only one desire, but the objects of desire change? Desire is always the same—perhaps fear is always the same—one fear which is translated into different fears. I am afraid of this and that, but I realize that fear cannot be divided. This is something that you have to realize, it is not a logical conclusion, not something which you put together and believe in. But when you see that fear cannot be divided you have made a discovery that is tremendous and then you will have put away altogether this problem of the unconscious and you will no longer depend on the psychologists, the analysts. This is really a very serious thing, for when you see that fear is indivisible you understand that it is a movement which expresses itself in different ways, not the separate fears of death, of my wife, of losing my job, of not achieving, fulfilling myself and so on. And as long as you see that movement—and not the object to which the movement goes—then you are facing an immense question. Then you are asking how one can look at fear which is indivisible and therefore not fragmentary, without the fragmentation which the mind has cultivated. You are following? I have been presented with the nature of fear as a totality, there is only a total fear, not the fragmentary fears. Now can my mind, which thinks in fragments—my wife, my child, my family, my job, my country—you know how it functions in fragments—can my fragmentary mind observe the total picture of fear? Can it? You are understanding the question? I have lived a life of fragmentation, my thought is only capable of thinking in fragmentation, so I only look at fear through the fragmentary process of thought. To look at total fear must I not be without the fragmentary process of thought? Thought, the whole process of the machinery of thinking, is fragmentation, it breaks up everything. I love you and I hate you, you are my enemy, you are my friend. My peculiar idiosyncrasies, my inclinations are in battle with everything else—my job, my position, my prestige, my country and your country, my God and your God—it is all the fragmentation of thought. And this thought is always old, it is never new and is therefore never free. Thought can never be free because it is the reaction of memory and memory is old. This thought looks at the total state of fear, or tries to look at it, and when it looks it reduces it into fragments. So the mind can only look at this total fear when there is no movement of thought.

We will proceed the day after tomorrow, because there is much to be gone into. Can we discuss, what we have talked about this morning?

Questioner: Sir, you take a fundamental question like fear and you have the confidence to approach that problem, *even though it sounds like analysis. I am sure it doesn't bother you a bit—you approach it with full confidence. Now what is that confidence and how does it arise? How does one go about it?*

KRISHNAMURTI: How do you know I have confidence? And what do you mean by that word "confidence?" You say I have confidence in approaching a problem of such a nature as fear. Is it confidence? That is to say, being certain, capable, being capable of analysis, capable of seeing the whole of it—having the capacity and from that capacity having confidence; because you are sure and confident in yourself—you are clever and therefore you can tackle such a fundamental issue. And you ask, how do I get that confidence? First you posit, you state that I have confidence, then you ask how do I get it? How do you know I have confidence? Perhaps I have no confidence at all? Do follow this please. I dislike or distrust confidence for it implies that one is certain, and has achieved; one moves as from a platform, from a state, which means one has accumulated a great deal of knowledge, a great deal of experience and from that one has gained confidence and is therefore able to tackle the problem. But it isn't a bit like that, quite the contrary, for the moment one has reached a conclusion, a position of achievement, of knowledge, from which one starts examining, one is finished, then one is translating every living thing in terms of the old. Whereas, if one has no foothold, if there is no certainty, no achievement, then there is freedom to examine, freedom to look. And when one looks with freedom it is always new.

A man who is confident is a dead human being, like the priest, like the commissar, believing in ideologies, in God, in their conclusions, their ideas, their reactions; they have produced a hideous, monstrous world. Whereas a man who is free to look, and look without the background—without having any opinion, any conclusion, without any standard or principle—he can observe and his observation is always clear, unconfused, fresh and innocent. It is that innocency alone that can see the totality of this whole process.

67

Questioner: Sir, there is an essential difference; that is, you approach this whole problem and you don't ask anybody about it at all, and I don't do that. What is the nature of what you do?

KRISHNAMURTI: The problem is not the essential difference between the speaker and the questioner, but why does the questioner depend? Why do you depend, what are the implications of dependence? I depend on my wife, or my wife depends on me—why? Follow this out—don't brush it aside. Why does she depend on me? Is it not because in herself she is not clear, she is unhappy, therefore I help her, I sustain her, I nourish her, or she nourishes me. So it is a mutual dependence, psychologically as well as objectively. So I depend, and when she looks at somebody else she has taken away that support on which I depend, I am hurt, I am afraid, I am jealous. So if you depend on me, on the speaker, to nourish you psychologically, then you will always be in doubt and say, "My goodness, he may be wrong" or "There is a better teacher round the corner, there is a greater psychologist, the latest anthropologist who has studied so much, who knows so much." So you will depend on him; but if you understand the nature of your own dependence then you will have no need of authority at all from anybody. Then your eyes will be clear to look; then you will really look out of innocence and innocence is its own action.

18th July 1967

6

WE WILL CONTINUE: talking over together the whole complex problem of fear. I think we should bear in mind that we are concerned not merely about the peripheral changes but rather with a radical revolution in the very psyche itself; we must understand the psychological structure not only of the society in which we live, but also the psychological structure and the nature of ourselves. The two, society and ourselves, are not separate. We are society and living in a world that is so confused, so antagonistic and at war, we must bring about a revolution in ourselves—that's the primary issue at all times. The more one is concerned, not merely with superficial change, with the world, with its misery, with its devilment, but really concerned with one's own structure and nature, the more it seems to me one must become very, very serious. We are serious about certain things which give us a great deal of pleasure, a great deal of satisfaction, we want to pursue that pleasure at any price, whether it be sexual or the fulfilment of ambition, or some kind of gratification. But very few of us are serious in the sense of seeing the whole problem of existence, the conflicts, the wars, the anxieties, the despairs, the loneliness, the suffering. To be serious about these fundamental issues means a continual attention to these matters, not just sporadic interest, not an interest that you occasionally give when you have a problem that is biting you. This seriousness must be our background, from which we think, live and act; otherwise we fritter away our life discussing endlessly things that really don't matter, which is such a waste of energy. The more one is serious inwardly, the more there is maturity. Maturity is not a matter of age, surely? It is not a matter of gathering a great many experiences, or accumulating a great deal of knowledge. Maturity has nothing to do with age and time, but comes rather with this quality of seriousness. Such maturity is only possible when there is wider and deeper knowing of oneself.

This quality of maturity—must it be left to time, to circumstances, to inclination, or to a particular form of tendency? Is it like a fruit that ripens during the summer and is ready to fall in the autumn, taking time, many days of rain, sunshine, cloudy weather, and cold, and then after all the adversity of climate it is ready to be taken away? Is this maturity a matter of adversity? I feel there is no time to waste and that one must be mature immediately, not biologically or physiologically, but mature inwardly, completely ripe totally. Is that a matter of adversity, experience, knowledge, time and so on? I think this is an important question to ask of ourselves, because unfortunately we mature rather too early, biologically and die physically before we have understood the whole meaning of life.

We spend our days in regret, in remembrances, in building images about ourselves. Will this bring about maturity —or is maturity something that is immediate, not touched by time at all? Do please ask yourself this question—because we are here not just to listen to talks, to endless discussions, verbal exchange and the piling up of words, but we are here, it seems to me, and I say this with humility,

70

not to accumulate knowledge and experience, but rather to see things directly and immediately, as they are. I feel that in that lies the quality of maturity in which there is no deception, no dishonesty, no double thinking, no double standard. We are here to see ourselves actually as we are, without any fear, without the images which we have built about ourselves; each one of us has an image of what we should be, we have an idea that we are great, or very uninteresting, dull or mediocre—or, we have a feeling that we are extraordinarily affectionate, superior, full of wisdom, knowledge. These pictures we have of ourselves deny totally the perceiving of the immediate, of "what is." There is a conflict between the image and "what is," and it seems to me that maturity is a state of mind in which the image is not and there is only "what is," in that there is no conflict whatsoever. A mind that is in conflict is not mature, whether the conflict be with the family, with oneself, with desires, with one's ambitions, one's fulfilments. Conflict at any level surely indicates a mind that is not mature, ripe, clear. A mind that is always seeking, demanding, hoping, can never mature.

When discussing together this question of fear, we must bear in mind that it is not just a fear, not just a particular form of fear, in which one is caught, but that it is fear itself, which is expressed in different ways. Desire changes its object; when one is young, one wants all kinds of enjoyable, pleasurable, sensual things, and as one grows older desire changes its object, it gets more and more complex, but it is still the same desire although the object of that desire changes. In the same way there is only fear, not the varieties of fears. When we go into this question of fear, we must bear in mind that one must see the totality of fear and not the fragmentation of fear. One may be afraid of the neighbor, of the wife, of death, of loneliness, of old age, of never having loved, or never knowing what love is and never knowing what this sense of complete abandonment is, because it is only in the total abandonment of oneself that there is beauty. Not knowing all this, one is afraid, not only of the known but also of the

71

unknown. One must consider fear totally, not the fragmentary fears in which one is caught.

The question then is—can one perceive the totality of fear? Can one see fear completely, and not its various aspects? I may be afraid of death and you may be afraid of loneliness, another may be afraid of not becoming famous, or living a life which is so boring, lonely, drugged, weary, a routine. One may be afraid of so many things, and we are apt to wish that we could solve each fear by itself, one by one. Such a wish seems to me, to be immature, for there is only fear.

Can the mind see the totality of fear and not merely the different forms of fear? You understand my question? Now how is it possible to see the totality of fear as well as these different aspects of it—the central structure and nature of fear and also its fragmentation, such as the fear of the dark, the fear of walking alone, the fear of the wife or the husband, or losing the job? If I could understand the central nature of fear then I should be able to examine all the details, but if I merely look at the details then I shall never come to the central issue.

Most of us, when there is fear, are apt to run away from it, or suppress it, control it, or turn to some form of escape. We do not know how to look. We do not know how to live with that fear. Most of us are, unfortunately, afraid of something, from childhood until we die; living in such a corrupt society, the education that we receive engenders this fear. Take your particular kind of fear, if you are at all aware, watch your reactions, look at it, look at it without any movement of escape, justification, or suppression, just look at it. I may have a particular fear of disease, can I look at it without any tremor, without any escape, without any hope—just look at it?

I think the "how to look" is very important. The whole problem lies in the words "to look, to see and to listen." Can I look at a fear without the word that causes that fear? Can I look without the word which arouses fear, like the word "death"? The word itself brings a tremor, an anxiety, just as the word "love" has its own tremor, its own image.

Can I look at that fear without the word, without any reaction, justification, or acceptance, or denial; can I just look at it? I can only look when the mind is very quiet, just as I can only listen to what you are saying when my mind is not chattering to itself, carrying on a dialogue with itself—only then can I listen to what you are saying completely. If I am carrying on my own conversation, with my own problems, my own anxieties, I am incapable of listening to you. In the same way can I look at a fear, or a problem that I have, can I just look at it, without trying to solve it, without trying to build courage and all the rest, can I merely observe it? One can observe a cloud, a tree or a movement of the river with a fairly quiet mind because it is something that is not very important to each one of us, but when there is fear, despair, when one is directly in contact with loneliness, with jealousy, with an ugly state of that kind, then can one just look at it so completely, one's mind so quiet, that one can really see?

A quiet mind is not to be cultivated; a mind that is made to be quiet is a stagnant mind, it has no quality of depth, width and beauty. But when you are serious you want to see fear completely, you no longer want to live with fear for it is a dreadful thing; you have had fear, you must know how it warps, twists, how it darkens the days. When you become serious, intense, it is like living with a serpent in your room, you watch every movement, you are very, very sensitive to the least noise it makes. To observe fear you have to live with it, you must know and understand all its content, its nature, its structure, its movement. Can one live with fear in this way? Have you ever tried living in this way with anything, living with yourself first, living with your wife or husband? If you have tried living with yourself you begin to see that "yourself" is not a static state, it is a living thing—to live with that living thing your mind must also be alive, it cannot be alive if it is caught in opinions, judgments and values. To live with a living thing is one of the most difficult things to do, for we do not live with the living thing but with the image and the image is a

73

dead thing to which we continually add and that is why all relationships go wrong.

To live with fear, which is alive, requires a mind and a heart that are extraordinarily subtle, that have no conclusion, no formula and therefore can follow every movement of fear. If you so observe and live with fear—and this doesn't take a whole day, it can take a second, a minute—you begin to know the whole nature of fear and you will inevitably ask: who is the entity that is living with fear, who is it that is living with it, following it, that is observing it? Who is the "observer" and what is he observing?

You are asking yourself—who is the observer, who is it that is living, watching and taking into account all the movements of the various forms of fear and is also aware of the central fact of fear? Is the observer a dead entity, a static being—has he not accumulated a lot of knowledge and information about himself, learnt so much, had so many experiences—is not all this experience, this knowledge, this infinite variety of loneliness and suffering, the past, a dead thing, memory; is it not a dead thing that observes and lives with the movement of fear? Is the observer the static dead past or a living thing? What is your answer? Are you the dead entity that is watching a living thing; or a living thing watching a living thing? In the observer the two states exist—when you observe a tree, you observe with the botanical knowledge of that tree and also you observe the living movement of that tree, the wind on the leaves, among the branches, how the trunk moves with the wind; it is a living thing and you are looking at it with accumulated knowledge about that tree and that knowledge is a dead thing—or, you look at it without any accumulated knowledge, so that you, who are a living thing, are looking at a living thing. The observer is both the past and the living present—the observer is the past, which touches the living present.

Let us bring it much nearer. When you, who are the observer, look at your wife, your friend, are you observing with the memories of yesterday, are you aware that yesterday is contaminating the present—or, are you observing as

74

though there were no yesterday at all? The past is always overshadowing the present, the past memory—what she said to me, what he said to me—the pleasure, the flattery of yesterday, the insult of yesterday, these memories touch the present and give it a twist. The observer is both the past and the present, he is half alive and half dead, and with this life and death he looks.

Is there an observer who is neither of the past nor of the present, in terms of time? That there is the observer who is of the past, is fairly clear—the image, the symbol, the idea, the ideologies and so on, the past—yet he is also actively present, actively examining, looking, observing, listening. That listening, that looking is touched by the past and the observer is still within the field of time. When he observes the object, fear, or whatever it is, within the field of time, he is not seeing the totality of fear. Now can the observer go beyond, so that he is neither the past nor the present, so that the observer is the observed, which is the living? This, that we are talking about, is real meditation.

It is very difficult to express in words the nature of that state of mind in which there is not only the past as the observer, but also the observer who is actually observing, listening and yet with a chapter, a root in the past. It is because the observer lives in the past and in the present which is touched by the past, that there is a division between the observer and the observed. This division, this space, this time interval, between the observer and the observed, comes to an end only when there is another quality, which is not of time at all, which is neither of the past nor of the present; then only is the observer the observed, and this is not a process of identification with the observed.

I was told by someone who had studied these things, that in ancient China, before a painter of nature commenced to paint, he sat in front of a tree for days, months, years—it doesn't matter—until he was the tree; not that he became the tree, not that he identified himself with the tree, but he was the tree. This means that there was no space between the observer and the observed, there was no experience as

75

the observer experiencing the beauty, the movement, the shadow, the depth of a leaf, the quality of color. He was totally the tree and only in that state could he paint. In ancient India this also existed, they were not trying to be fashionable, non-objective, non this and that and all the modern tricks. Identification with something is fairly easy but it leads to greater conflict, misery, and loneliness. Most of us identify ourselves with the family, with the husband, with the wife, the nation, and that has led to great misery, great wars. We are talking of something entirely different and you must understand this, not verbally, but at the core, in your heart, right at the root of your being, then you will see that you will be for ever timelessly free of fear, and only then will you know what love is.

One must understand the observer and not the thing observed, for that has very little value. Fear has very little value actually if you come to think of it; what has value is how you look at fear, what you do with fear or what you do not do with fear. The analysis, the seeking of the cause of fear, the everlasting questioning, asking, dreaming, all that is of the observer, so that understanding the observer has a greater value than understanding the observed. As one looks at the observer, which is oneself, one sees that oneself is not only of the past, as the dead memories, hopes, guilt, knowledge, but that all knowledge is in the past. When one says "I know", one means, "I know you as you were yesterday; I don't know you actually now." Oneself is the past, living in the present touched by the past, over-shadowed by the past, and tomorrow is waiting, which also is part of the observer. All that is within the field of time in the sense of yesterday, today and tomorrow. That is all one knows and with this state of mind, as the observer, one looks at fear, at jealousy, at war, at the family—that enclosing entity called the family—and with that one lives. The observer is always trying to solve the problem of the thing which is observed, which is the challenge, which is the new, and one is always translating the new in terms of the old, one is everlastingly, until one comes to an end, in conflict.

One cannot understand intellectually, verbally, argumen-

76

tatively, or through explanations, a state of mind in which the observer has no longer the space between himself and the thing observed, in which the past is no longer interfering, at any time, yet it is only then that the observer is the observed and only then that fear comes totally to an end.

As long as there is fear there is no love. What is love? There are so many explanations of love, as sex, as belonging to somebody, being not dominated by somebody, being nourished psychologically by another, all the thinking about sex; it is all generally understood as love—and there is always anxiety, fear, jealousy, guilt. Surely where there is such conflict there is no love. This is not an aphorism to learn but rather a fact to observe in oneself; do what you will, as long as there is fear, as long as there is any form of jealousy, anxiety, you cannot possibly love. Love has nothing whatsoever to do with pleasure and desire—pleasure goes with fear, and a mind that lives in fear must obviously always be seeking pleasure. Pleasure only increases fear, so one is caught in a vicious circle. By being aware of that vicious circle, just by watching it, living with it, never trying to find a way out of it—for the circle is broken not because you are doing something about it—you will break that circle. Then only when there is no pleasure, no desire or fear, then there is something called love.

Questioner: *It seems to me that fear is necessary to our self-protection.*

KRISHNAMURTI: Yes Sir, that's fairly clear isn't it? Physically, fear is directly related to biological existence. As long as one must have physical security there must be fear.

Obviously that is true. As long as I depend on somebody for food and shelter I must be afraid, physically, of not having food and shelter tomorrow. But modern society— the welfare society—sees that one has food and shelter and clothing. Even though I may have food, clothes, and shelter, which are absolutely necessary, yet beyond that there is fear because I want to be secure psychologically. I want to be secure in my relationship with another, in my position which I have built as of the most extraordinary importance, a position which gives me a status, a regard from others; so there are not only physical fears but also psychological fears. The psychological fears have created a society which sustains or maintains the physical fears. The psychological fears come into being when we are German, French, English, Russian, with our nationalism, our stupid flags, with our kings and queens and separate armies and all that immaturity. That nonsense is destroying us. We are spending millions and millions on armaments and in destroying others. There is no security for us, physically even; not so much here in Switzerland, or in Holland, or in England, but go to India, go to the Middle East, go to Vietnam—for the great insecurity there, we are all responsible. What is of first importance, is to understand and therefore go beyond, above, the psychological securities, the vested interests which we have in nationalities, in the family, in religions and all the rest; then we shall have physical security and there will be no wars.

Questioner: How is it that the dead past has such an overwhelming influence over the actual present?

KRISHNAMURTI: How is it that the dead past has such control over the thing which I think is living—I think it is living? But is it living—or are we only the dead past, to which we are trying to give life, in the present? Which means, are you living—you understand—living? You may eat, you may have sexual experience, you may climb the mountains, but all those are mechanical actions. But are you actually living, or is it the past living in the present so that you are not living at all—the past continuing in the present, giving it a quality of living? I don't know if you have ever observed yourself—what is, "yourself"? There is "yourself" which is the dead weight of the past and you say you are living in the present. What is the thing that says— "I am living", that consciousness that says—"I am alive"— apart from the physical organism that has its own responses, its own motivation? What is the thing that says—"I am alive"—is it thought, is it feeling? If it is thought, obviously thought is always the old—if you really saw that thought is always the old, if you really saw it as you feel hunger, then you would see that what you think is living is only a modified continuation of the past, it is thinking. Is there any other living thing?—not God in you, which again is another form of thought, thought having invented God, because thought in itself is so uncertain, so dead that it has to invent a living thing—is there really a living thing, living independently of any motive, any stimulation, any dependence; is there a living thing that is not subject to circumstances, to tendencies, to inclination? Go into yourself and you will find out—find out, and if you can live with what you have found out, then perhaps you will be able to go beyond it and come upon something that is timeless living.

20th July 1967

7

WE WERE SAYING the other day that fear and being beyond and above fear, is a very complex problem, it needs a great deal of understanding in which there is neither suppression nor control nor any form of elimination. To understand fear one must be aware of the structure and the nature of fear—one has to learn about it and not come to it with any form of conclusion.

I do not know if you have thought about the question of learning. It is really quite an interesting issue. What is learning—and do we ever learn? Do we learn from experience? Do we ever learn from accumulation of knowledge? We say we learn from experience—do we? There have been nearly fifteen thousand wars during the last five thousand years—that is a great deal of experience for man. Have we learnt from these experiences that war is a most appalling thing and must come to an end? And is learning a matter of time? We have not learnt after five thousand years that war, the organized killing of another, for whatever reason, is a most ... I don't know what words to use. If we have not learnt during these five thousand years then is learning a matter of time? Apparently we have not learnt from this vast experience of killing another—what will teach us? Apparently environmental circumstances, pressures, disturbances, destruction, starvation, brutality, have not taught us and we have taken five thousand years to learn that we haven't learnt. So what is learning? Please, this is quite a serious question, this is not a schoolboy question which is put in a school for an essay. What is learning and when does it take place—is it a matter of time, a gradual process? And enquiring about learning and whether it implies time, I think we have to enquire into the question of humility. In talking of humility we are talking not of the harshness of the saint or the priest or of the vain man who cultivates humility. Obviously if I want to learn about something my mind must not have reached any conclusion about it, it must have no opinion or previous knowledge. It is only a mind that is very innocent that can enquire into the question of humility—innocent in the sense that it is not knowing and is capable of a great deal of freedom. Obviously learning has nothing whatsoever to do with the accumulation of knowledge or experience or tradition and it is only a mind that is free that can be in a state of humility—it is only such a mind that can learn. And with such an act of learning one can approach the very complex problem of fear. And you cannot learn about fear because you have heard here a series of explanations which you apply, for that application is merely mechanical and therefore fails to act. So when we begin to understand—for ourselves and not according to somebody else—what humility is, that it is a mind that is not cluttered up with opinions, judgements, knowledge, then there is a state in which we are capable of learning.

Look Sirs, what we are talking over together is a very serious matter, it is not entertainment, not something that you casually hear out of curiosity and pass it by. Either you listen attentively, or not at all. Much better not to listen, much better to go out for a walk in the rain, if you like the rain, enjoy yourself among the trees, but if you are here do pay complete attention, because what we are discussing is a very serious matter. What is implied in all this is a total psychological revolution which lies beyond society; and the bringing about of a radical revolution in the psyche of the individual himself; we are only concerned with a total mutation of the individual, for the individual is the collective, the two are not separate. As society is the individual and the individual is society, then to bring about a transformation within the structure of society the individual must completely change. And this is what we are talking about and in doing so we are finding out and learning about this total mutation. But to learn, not to repeat, not to go on with explanations and dialectical arguments and opinions, but to actually learn, requires a great deal of humility. Most of us, unfortunately, have conclusions, opinions, judgments, beliefs, dogmas, from which we evaluate from which we start, that is to say, a platform from which we live. Such a mind can never possibly learn, just as man has not learnt through wars what appalling things are involved in killing another! We haven't learnt. So to learn one must start with great humility. If one has opinions, conclusions, definite dogmas, one is merely accumulating, therefore resisting, and hence creating conflict in oneself and with another, which is society.

So, is learning a matter of time? Is humility to be cultivated? Humility is freedom and it is only in freedom you can learn, not with an accumulation of memories. Can humility be a matter of cultivation and therefore of time? Can humility be acquired gradually? Please see what is implied in it, for if it is a matter of time in which to accumulate humility, then humility is being cultivated—the moment you have cultivated or gathered humility it ceases to be humility. Obviously, a man who says "I am humble" is a most vain man. Humility is not of time, therefore it is not a matter of cultivation—it is a matter of instant perception and that immediate perception is denied when you make humility an idea.

You hear that it is only a very clear, innocent mind, that can learn, and you want to learn about fear. You hear that

82

and it has already become an idea—you want to be free from fear and you hear that you must learn about it and can only learn if your mind is very clear, simple—this structure has already become an organized thought, an idea. From that idea you hope you are going to learn, but you are not learning at all, you are merely carrying an idea into action and between idea and action there is conflict. You do not, in that, see instantly the truth of learning, the truth of humility, in which the very seeing is the acting. I think we must go over this in different ways so that it becomes very clear.

Have you ever wondered why you have ideas and opinions at all—why? Why do you form an image, an image being an idea? Why does thought function through ideas, ideas of nationality, of what is right and what is wrong, that it is right to kill under certain circumstances, the beliefs that you have about God, the family and the non-family; you have ideas—why? Are ideas a means of self-protection, a resistance to any form of change, to any form of movement, to life? And do ideas—psychological ideas, not technical ideas, I am not talking about them—do ideas bring about clarity of action? Or are not these ideas always the past—and for this reason is not the past always acting in the present and continuing in the future? I learn a trade, having learnt that particular trade, that particular function, I then proceed to apply what I have learnt. Then that which I have learnt and according to which I act becomes mechanical, repeated over and over again. That gives me a sense of security, in which there is no disturbance; I can add more to it, but it will always be mechanical.

So there are several things involved in learning. Do we learn ideas, conclusions and having learnt them, apply them in action? That is one of the things. And is there idea separate from action at the moment when you are acting? Are all ideas—whether the Christian ideas, or Communists', Socialists', Capitalists' ideas, whatever they are—are all ideas in the past? All ideas are always in the past, therefore when I am functioning according to ideas, dogmas, be-

83

liefs, conclusions, I am living in the past, therefore I am dead. It is as if a man lived on dead memories. Is there at the moment you are doing—not having learnt and then doing, but as you are actually doing—is there at that moment idea? That is to say, I am angry or I am jealous, at that moment of anger or jealousy is there idea? Or is idea a judgment about anger which I have formed in the past and with which I condemn anger, or justify anger?

Learning implies a great sensitivity and there is no sensitivity if there is an idea, which is of the past, dominating the present. It is only a very sensitive mind that can learn and that sensitivity is denied when there is the domination of an idea. That is, as a Communist with all the Marxian-Leninist doctrines, or with all the learning and the accumulated ideas of the bourgeois, or with dialectical ideas and so on. I am no longer sensitive, the mind is no longer quick, pliable, alert—it is incapable of learning. Learning implies humility and in that state a mind cannot be achieving—the moment you achieve you cease to have that quality of innocency and humility. And there can be a mind that is clear, that is sensitive, not only physically sensitive but much more important, a mind which is psychologically sensitive, inwardly, inside the skin. Most of us are insensitive, even physically. Do observe yourselves. We overeat, we have not thought about the right diet, we over-smoke, so that our bodies become gross, insensitive, the quality of attention in the organism itself is made dull. How can there be a very sensitive mind, alert, clear, if the organism itself is dull, heavy? We may be sensitive about certain things which touch us personally, but to be sensitive totally, to all the implications of life, demands non-fragmentation of the organism as separate from the psyche, a total movement, a unitary movement.

To learn about fear is to learn about sorrow, also to learn about fear is to learn about pleasure. Pleasure and fear go together. If I don't get what I want I am frightened, I am anxious, I am jealous, I become hateful. To understand fear one must understand sorrow—I think the two are related. Yet before we enter into the question of sorrow we must understand passion. I am sorry there are so many things to understand, life is like that, isn't it, really? It isn't that one thing is understood and then you hope to understand everything else. But there is really only one thing to understand and if you do understand that completely everything else is of little importance. But to come upon that totality requires not only a non-fragmentary mind but also a great deal of love.

We must understand and learn about fear and learning about fear means learning about sorrow and the ending of sorrow and all this implies the enquiry into passion. You know that word is derived from sorrow, and most of us consciously, or otherwise, are in sorrow of some kind or another. We are sorrowful human beings who have not a moment of bliss *uncontaminated by thought*, not a moment of real deep enjoyment *untouched by any thought or memory*. We are a battlefield from the moment we are born until we die. There is never order, never peace, never a sense of tranquillity and bliss. All that we know is sorrow and conflict.

To understand the nature of sorrow we must, as we said, go into this question of passion. You know, love is not desire or pleasure and that is a very difficult thing to see the truth of—to see, to actually feel from the very depth of your being, that love is not desire or pleasure. Because desire, which we have gone into in previous talks, becomes pleasure through thinking about something which has given you pleasure, enjoyment, and you think about it more and more—that thought is not love. Thinking about you, whom I love, is not love. When I think about you—whom I think I love—when I think about you, it is pleasure that I have derived from you being sustained by thought—I think about you and *the moment thought enters love goes away*. What we know of love, as desire, pleasure and passion, which is lust, has nothing whatsoever to do with the passion which we are talking about, which passion is not the product of thought. If I become passionate about you, about something or an idea, it has stimulation in it, it has motive in it, the motive being "I am going to derive

85

pleasure." Please watch in yourself all this. So passion through, or for, something, is not the passion we are talking about, because in all that is involved pain and sorrow. Passion implies that thought and idea have been totally abandoned. And when there is that passion, that intensity, that drive—which is always in the present, not tomorrow or yesterday—then we can come upon this question of sorrow and see whether it can ever end.

A mind that is in sorrow cannot possibly function naturally, it becomes neurotic, it may take to the various drugs, whether STP or LSD or marihuana, because it hasn't understood life, life has no meaning for it and life is very superficial. If by the time you are twenty you have had everything, then you want more of the so-called mind-expanding drugs that give you heightened sensitivity for the time being, but they do not free the mind from sorrow.

So what we are trying to do, or trying to talk over together, is to see if it is at all possible to completely end sorrow. You know, there is the sorrow of loneliness, there is the sorrow of death, there are all those petty little sorrows of not having love or not having been loved, or not being able to fulfil, not being a great man, the quantities of sorrows that we accumulate through life. Is it possible to be free, of the great and the little sorrows, of all sorrow? Is it possible to sweep them all away? It is only possible when there is that passion to find out and that passion does find out through self-knowing—through learning about oneself but not according to Freud, Jung and the psychologists and analysts, that is too infantile, for if I learn according to them I learn what they are, I am not learning about myself. To learn about myself there must be no moment of accumulation from which I learn. Myself is a constant movement, of yesterday through to today and tomorrow, a single movement, endless. I have to learn about this movement and I can only learn if the mind is free from all previous conclusions about myself. To see that on the instant, to see this whole movement, you must have intense passion. When you listened to the thunder last night—if you listened and were not too heavily asleep—if you listened and if there was space between the listener and the thing that you listened to, you didn't hear the thunder. But if you listened without any idea, directly, then you were the thunder, because there was no space between you and that. This is not some fantastic, oriental rubbish. You know, life being divided into the Orient and the Occident is really very immature, we are human beings whether we live in India or China or in this lovely country. And man is in sorrow, has always been in sorrow and because he does not know how to get out of it, how to end sorrow, he worships it personified in a church—therefore you must have the redeemer, a savior and all the rest of the things that man has invented when he finds himself in sorrow and there is no way out. But we are saying that there is a way out, completely and totally, and that is to see the total movement of life as yourself, on the instant, and to see that clearly you must have passion. There is no passion when there is fear, you do not have passion when there is love, which is not desire or pleasure.

Can we talk over together what we have said this morning?

Questioner: Sir, you said that to learn we must have a sensitive mind, but when we have not a sensitive mind how do you get it?

KRISHNAMURTI: First, does one know that one's mind is not clear and sensitive? Do you know it? Please follow carefully? Do you know this as you know hunger? Or do you know it because somebody has told you or because you are comparing your mind with somebody else's and you say to yourself "My mind is not clear"? You see the difference? Do you compare and therefore say "I am not"? When you compare, what is taking place? You have an idea that you are dull and you have an idea that somebody else is very intelligent. The two images, the one about yourself and the image about another, are in competition. Can you observe yourself as being dull without comparison? Or do you know only through comparison? Now this is an important question to ask and to answer. Do you know that you are hungry because you were hungry yesterday, or do you know hunger because you are actually hungry? You know through comparison and you don't really know, or do you know because it is so? This is a very important question because throughout life, from childhood, from school until we die, we are taught to compare ourselves with another; yet when I compare myself with another I am destroying myself. In a school, in an ordinary school where there are a lot of boys, when one boy is compared with another, who is very clever, who is the head of the class, what is actually taking place? You are destroying the boy. That's what we are doing throughout life. Now, can I live without comparison—without comparison with anybody? This means there is no high, no low—there is not the one who is superior and the other who is inferior. You are actually what you are and to understand what you are, to look at yourself and to see actually what you are, this process of comparison must come to an end. If I am always comparing myself with some saint or some teacher, some business-man, writer, poet, and all the rest, what has happened to me—what have I done? I only compare in order to gain, in order to achieve, in order to become—but when I don't compare I am beginning to understand what I am. Beginning to understand what I am is far more fascinating, far more interesting, it goes beyond all this stupid comparison.

Questioner: What does it mean, to be serious, and why am I not serious?

KRISHNAMURTI: Sir, very few people are serious, anyhow. We are serious at odd moments, when we are driven into a corner. What does it mean to be serious, Sir, to you, to each one of us—what does it mean? It means, generally, that we become serious when there is a personal threat, danger—when our security, financial or emotional, or our security in relationship, is disturbed—then we become very serious. That seriousness turns to jealousy, fear, self-protection. *Is that really seriousness?* To be serious means

to be earnest doesn't it? not merely sincere or integrated—
to be earnest about life, about earning a living, the family,
what you do, what you think, what you feel, to be serious
about the totality of all that. To be earnest, serious, not
when you are forced, not when you are pricked, not when
you have some profit to gain or some pleasure to achieve.
This seriousness is not to be given by another, for then it is
merely a stimulation—and if you are being stimulated to be
serious this morning, in this gathering, then when you go
outside it will evaporate.

23rd July 1967

8

WE WERE TALKING of being serious. I do not think one can be serious about this and not serious about that—one can only be serious about everything, from the most trivial things that you do to the most profound problems of life. One cannot be casual about anything, for a casual mind is really a very frivolous mind, choosing what it will be serious about for a few days or a few years and then moving from that to other forms of seriousness. Whereas if one is actually serious about everything—and I mean everything, from the shape of your hand to the most deeply perplexing problems of life—then that quality of seriousness pervades throughout one's life, not only when one is young but right through as one becomes older. And it seems to me that a mind that is quick in offering opinions, a mind that flits about from one idea to another, or from one experience to another, from one sexual appetite to another—such a mind is obviously not very serious. Such a mind will not only have more and more problems, but also it cannot possibly understand the very complex problem of life.

We have also been talking about fear and we shall continue enquiring, not only into the structure and the nature of fear, but also to find out whether one can actually be deeply and profoundly free from that thing we call fear. Because it seems to me that unless you leave at the end of these talks actually free, entirely, right through your being, of this enormous weight of fear—and not with more problems, not with more complex desires to understand what has been said, not caught in explanations—then it seems to me that your attending the talks will be utterly useless, will have no meaning and these gatherings will become another form of entertainment, another form of stimulation and every form of stimulation makes the mind more dull, more heavy, incapable of swift movement.

You must be well aware of what is actually happening in the world, not only in your little family, but right through the world: in Asia, in America and in Europe. There is a revolt against the established order because what is called established order is nothing very great. What has the older generation built, for which, please bear in mind, each one of us is responsible? Each one of us is responsible for every war, whether it is in the East, or in Europe, or in America or elsewhere—each one of us is responsible for the confusion, for the misery, for the ugliness that is going on in the world. When we emphasize the individual it is not an emphasis of the individual as opposed to society. A very serious man is neither an individual nor concerned with society, he is outside both the field of individuality and the structure of society, he is entirely a different human being. The individual is the society, and the society is the individual—they are indivisible.

We went into it very carefully during these talks and saw how each one of us—I most intensely feel this, it is not mere lip service or just words—how each one of us is tremendously, insistently, responsible. And what have we built as society? There are still wars and it is a society in which the most important thing is success, big business, the churches. There are the religions that have no meaning whatsoever—listening to their rigmarole, their ideas, smell

91

their incense and everything else, you realize they have lost completely any meaning they ever had; naturally every intelligent man must be in revolt against the established, organized religious conceptions.

What are the young to do—join the army to kill and be killed—join big business and endlessly for the next forty years go to a wretched little office? Or shall they join the church—or take up in revolt, psychedelic drugs? What has this society to offer? Do look at it. What have you, who belong to this society, to this culture, what have you to offer? And look at the education that one has received, trained to be a lot of monkeys, to fit into a certain groove, a cog, become a technician, an expert in computers, capable of doing mechanical things. And for all this chaos and misery we are responsible. And this confusion, this misery, this personal achievement of which we are so very proud—whether in the field of literature, or going to the moon, or on the battlefield, killing more people and getting decorated for it, the constant misery, the turmoil, the anxiety, the utter hopeless despair of modern life—this whole field we call living. Isn't it so? Do observe it please, not as the speaker wishes, or as the speaker's particular prejudices or point of view—which he has not—but merely observe what actually is taking place within yourself and outside of yourself, observe the culture in which you live, the desire for power, position, prestige, name, success and intermingled with it all this peculiar idea of spirituality, of finding God through mind expanding drugs and so on and on. This field in which there is turmoil, conflict in every form of relationship, breeding hatred, antagonism, brutality and endless wars—we call living. This field, this life, is all that we know. We have cultivated escapes from this field, escapes through alcohol, escapes through churches, escapes through literature, through music, through art. Being incapable of solving this enormous battle of existence, we are naturally frightened of life, and being frightened of life, as it is, we seek every form of escape. And as we ourselves don't understand this life—other than according to some saint, some savior, some Freudian or Jungian or anybody,

92

including the speaker—as we haven't understood this life, each one of us of ourselves, we are frightened. We are frightened of the known, which is our daily existence, our daily relationships, our daily pleasures of sex and of all the subtle forms of pleasure which only lead to more pain. And we try to cover up this fear, to run away from it, or suppress it, we do anything to get away from this life of everyday existence, because we are frightened—which is being frightened of living. And we are frightened also of the unknown, frightened of death, essentially frightened of what lies beyond tomorrow. So we are frightened of the known and of the unknown—and this is our daily life. I do not think we are exaggerating. I do not think we are emphasizing something which is not actually so, for it is the canvas on which we have painted the life that each one of us leads and in it there is no hope. Every form of philosophy, every form of theological concept is merely an escape from the actual reality. If we are at all serious we have to face this, not allow ourselves for a single minute to escape from this, from this actual fact of what actually is. To face it one must be extraordinarily fearless because the facing of it involves not only how to observe it—which we have dealt with previously—but also one has to look at the question of time.

It is very important to understand the problem of time. Confronted with fear of living, faced with this problem of existence in which life has no meaning at all as it is, one can invent meanings, one can substitute for the ugly a concept of the beautiful, an ideological existence, but these are all escapes from actually what is. To understand, to resolve this life of misery, confusion and everything that one has contributed to make it so monstrous as it is, one has to understand not only how to observe but also understand the question of time. We are using the word "understanding," not in the sense of intellectual understanding or a verbal comprehension but as an understanding that comes when you give your whole attention to something. If I want to understand the beauty of a bird, a fly, or a leaf, or the nature of a person with all his complexities, I have

93

to give my attention. I can only give my attention completely when I really care to understand this problem, which means when I really love to understand it and am not frightened. In this understanding one has not only to know, observe, to learn about what it is to see, but also to learn about time and the process of thought—of what thinking is. With these things we have to be acquainted, familiar.

We have spoken of what it is to observe, to watch, to see, to listen. I do not think we are exaggerating when we say that very few of us ever do look—look at things outwardly or inwardly, look at ourselves, or objectively look at things. If I look at somebody whom I like, it is finished, I stop looking—if I look at somebody whom I don't like, I have also stopped looking because the like and dislike, which are a matter of reaction and opinion, judgement, prevent me from looking. Do follow this because if one doesn't understand this very simple, fundamental fact, we are not going to understand something which demands complete observation and attention.

Previous experience, previous knowledge, prevent you from looking, from listening. If you have hurt me, or if you have insulted me, then if I look at you with that memory I cannot see you. That is a very simple thing. What I look from is the insult, the image I have built about you, and that image, which is memory, which is idea, is looking at you, therefore I am not looking directly at you, therefore I am not listening to what you are saying at all, I am listening to my own whispers of my image about you. That is simple, but it becomes extraordinarily complex when you look at yourself. So that is the first thing to bear in mind, that one can look only when there is a freshness, when there is an innocency of mind, when there is a freedom to look. If that is somewhat clear, not verbally but actually, inwardly, for each one of us, then we can look at this question of time.

We are not talking about time by the watch—the train that goes by every morning at a particular time. We are talking about time in which there is the interval between idea and action. We have ideas such as those of non-violence—whether of the Communists, the Capitalists, or of the church-goers—we have ideas. There is idea and there is an interval between that idea and action. This interval between idea and action is time. Look at it—what is involved in that interval? The "idea" is to protect ourselves, obviously, it is the idea of being secure. But action is always immediate, action is not in the past or in the future—action means to act, it must be always in the present. And action is so dangerous, so uncertain, that we make it conform to an idea which will give us a certain satisfaction, pleasure, safety—there is thus an interval, thus conflict—isn't there? I have an idea of what is right or what is wrong, or an ideological concept about myself or about society, and according to that idea I will act. Therefore the action is in conformity with the idea, approximating itself to the idea, and hence always there is conflict. There is the idea, the interval and the action, and in the interval is the whole field of time.

We are enquiring whether time can come to an end, whether time can have a stop at all—which means, can conflict come to an end, not in the course of time, but immediately? If conflict is to come to an end during the course of time then you have the concept, or the idea, that conflict will come to an end, an idea that you are eventually going to achieve it. Therefore there is again an interval between concept and action—between the concept of non-violence and violence. There is the concept of non-violence and in that interval, which is time, you are sowing the seed of violence—obviously. That interval is essentially thought, therefore, is not time thought? By "time" we mean psychological time not chronological time—obviously. When you think you will be happy tomorrow, then you have an image of yourself achieving a result, of becoming happy tomorrow. It is thought, through desire and the continuity of that desire, as pleasure, sustained by thought, that says "tomorrow you will be happy", "tomorrow you will have success", "tomorrow the world will be the most beautiful world". So thought creates the interval, which is of time.

95

You can observe this in yourself. Look, you have had a pleasure, be it sexual or looking at a beautiful face or the shape of a lovely mountain and valley in the sun, you have enjoyed it, you have had a pleasure at that moment, an intense reaction—then thought comes in and says, "I'll keep it", "I'll store it up" and thought then says to itself, "When am I going to have it again, sex or other forms of pleasure?" So the idea of yesterday's pleasure is sustained by thought as something to be achieved again tomorrow—there is an interval—that interval is created by thought, which is time. Is this understood, not verbally, not analytically, not logically, but actually, inside you, is it so? If it is so, then the problem is—how to end it, how to put a stop to time? Because time is sorrow—yesterday, or a thousand yesterdays ago, I loved, or you loved, or you had a companion and he is gone, dead, and that memory remains and now you are thinking about that pleasure or that pain—you are thinking, looking back, wishing, hoping. That which you have enjoyed so greatly is denied, is absent, and thought, by thinking about it over and over again, breeds this thing that we call sorrow. So, also, as thought thinks over and over again about sex and its pleasure it creates further desire for pleasure and breeds not only sorrow but also gives continuity as time. Do see this in yourself, for as long as there is this interval of time bred by thought, there must be sorrow, there must be continuity of fear. So one asks oneself whether that interval, which is of time and of thought, can come to an end? Not tomorrow—you understand—for if we say, "Will it ever end?", it is already an idea which you want to achieve and therefore you have an interval, therefore you are caught again.

It is really extraordinarily interesting to watch the operation of one's own thinking, just to observe that reaction which one calls thinking. Where does it spring from?—obviously from memory. Is there a beginning to thought at all? You are following all this, not intellectually, you are asking yourself—can I find out the beginning of thought, that is to say, the beginning of memory, because if you had no memory you would have no thought? What is the beginning of thought, is it important at all? To us thought is extraordinarily important, the more clever, cunning, subtle, the more you can express it—you know—the ideas, intellectual or otherwise which fill the books of the intellectuals, whether theological or non-theological, whether of St. Thomas or of Shankara or the intellectuals in the Far East, or in the sectarian religious field, or in the non-religious field, they have filled thousands of books with ideas and we worship those books and ideas, they have tremendous importance for us. We are so heavily conditioned. And when we talk of ideas we are attacking the very root of them, not just your few little ideas, but the whole formulation of ideas.

To us, thinking—ideas, ideals, to discuss, to dialectically offer opinions and so on—has become extraordinarily important and we are questioning this whole edifice—you understand—whether it is the edifice of the church with all its dogmas and beliefs, with its formulas of God, the Virgin Mary and the Savior. The Christian world and the Asiatic world each have their own structure, their own edifice, their own scaffold to reach the Gods, and when we talk about thought as idea and time we are questioning the whole thing.

As human beings living in this monstrously ugly society with all its brutalities, guilt and anxiety, fears, wars and despair, we are asking ourselves—can all this come to an end?—not as a hope, but as an actual fact. Can the mind be made fresh, new and innocent, so that it can look at this existence and bring about a different world altogether?

One sees that we have separated action from idea, and that, to us, ideas are far more important than action; but ideas are always of the past and action is always of the present—action which is living, is always the present. We are frightened of that living present, so the past as ideas becomes very important, therefore there is death.

One of the factors of life is death. We are frightened of living, of old age, disease, pain and the sorrow which we know from the moment we are born until we die, which we call living, and we are also frightened of something which we do not know, which we call death. This whole field is our life.

One can see how thought creates fear. Please go into it with me, not just following the speaker, but take the journey together, share the way of moving together. So, we are frightened of life and we are frightened of death, of the known and the unknown, and that fear is bred by thought. I have had experience, I have reached a certain status, a certain position, achieved certain knowledge, which gives me vitality, energy, drive and that whole momentum of thought sustains me and I am frightened to lose it. Anybody who threatens my achievement and success, my platform, I loathe, I hate, I am his enemy. Surely this is so obvious. Don't you know in your business, or when you are teaching, how, when anybody surpasses you, you are frightened, you are antagonistic?—and you talk about God, spiritual life, and all the rest of it, but in your heart there is venom. And you are frightened to lose that and you are frightened of something much greater which is to come, which is death. So you think about death—you think about it and by thinking about it you are creating that interval between living and that which you call death. This is simple enough. The things that you know, the pleasure, the joys, the entertainments, the knowledge, the experience, the achievements, the despairs, the conflicts, the dominations,—you know, the things to which you cling, your house, your petty little family, your little nation, you hold on to those with grim death because they are all you have. By thinking about them you create an interval between what you think, as an idea, is lasting, and the actual fact.

Thought breeds, through time, not only the fear of living but the fear of death and because death is something you don't know, thought says, "Let's postpone it, avoid it, keep it as far away as possible, don't think about it"—but you are thinking about it. When you say, "I won't think about it" you have already thought about it. You have thought out how to avoid it and you can avoid it, through the many escapes, the churches, gods, saviors, the resurrection and the idea that there is a permanent, eternal self in yourself

98

which India, Asia, has invented. That is, thought has cleverly said that there is a permanent, eternal self in yourself—which endlessly—but because thought thinks about it, it is not real, obviously. Thought has created the idea of an eternal self—the soul, the Atman—in order to find safety, hope, but what thought has thought about is already a second-hand thing, thought is always of the old. One is frightened of death because one has postponed it. So the problem arises of how to go beyond this so called living and the thing called death. Is there an actual separation between the two? You understand? To live so intensely is to die to everything of yesterday, obviously—all the pleasures, the knowledge, the opinions, the judgments, the stupid little achievements, to die to all that—to die to the family, to die to your achievements which have only brought such chaos in the world and such conflict within yourself, to die to all that. Then to die to that brings an intensity, brings about a state of mind in which the past has ceased and the future, as death, has come to an end. So the living is the dying—you cannot live if you do not die. But most of us are frightened because we want surety, because we want to continue the misery which we have known, the disease, the pain, the pleasure, the anxiety. Because we avoid, push away, death—thought pushes away death—there is fear of the known and fear of the un-known. When there is no interval between death and the living, then you know what it means to die, to die everyday to everything that one has. Then the mind becomes ex-traordinarily fresh, eager, attentive and innocent. When one dies to the thousand yesterdays, then living is dying. It is only in that state that time comes to an end and thought functions only where it is needed and not at any other level or at any other demand.

Questioner: Sir, if thought arises within me and is not some outside force invading the field of the mind then it would seem that I am not different from thought; and then it would seem that if I choose to I could think as I choose to or not think.

KRISHNAMURTI: Why do you divide the outside and the inside? Is your thought your own; or is our thought conditioned by the outside? Of course it is. You are born as a Christian, as a Communist, as a—you know, born in this world in a society, in a culture, that conditions you in a certain way—you are conditioned by the books you read, the radio, the television, the newspapers, the preachers and are you not being conditioned by me, by the speaker? Are you? I hope not. Because if you are being conditioned by the speaker then you are merely accepting ideas and opinions which is of no value at all.

We are talking of something entirely different—freedom. But that freedom cannot come about if you divide the world as between the me, the thinker, the thoughts which are my own, and the rest of the world as totally disconnected from me. You think the way you think because you are an American, a Swiss or an Indian. You have a particular culture in which you were born, you are conditioned, you are shaped. The Communists have brain-washed millions of people, tortured them to think in the way of a particular society, with its leader, the boss, the commissar, the man who knows—and the church has done exactly the same thing in the other way—so that the culture, tortured with wars, in which you are born, is part of you, you are society as well as the individual, you cannot separate the two. You are outside of all this only when there is no fear and you can know what love is. But as long as you remain within that field of the culture, of society, of greed, of envy, of achievement, you are not a free human being. You may think you have free will, but you are just part of this monstrous society, a conditioned human being.

Questioner: How does "dying immediately" come in?

KRISHNAMURTI: It is fairly simple—die to one pleasure, immediately. You have a pleasure, smoking or whatever it is, just die to it, without argument, motive, fear, judgment, control, just say "well, finished"—do it—and you will know what it means. Not only to a little pleasure, it is

100

fairly simple to give up a cigarette—I know for some to give up a cigarette or a drink or a drug is an enormous problem, because it is a narcotic that keeps them quiet, makes the mind dull so they do not have to think—but die to one pleasure without argument, without motive, for that is what you are going to do when you die, you can't argue with death. So if you die to one wish, to one pleasure, without reacting, without being caught in despair, you will know what it means to die immediately to your whole complex, contradictory, existence.

25th July 1967

9

I THINK WE HAVE sufficiently talked over the question of fear, but, of course, we could go into greater detail and explore more minutely, but we would still be left, if we have not already understood, with the problem with which we began, which was fear. Mere concern with the details of fear does not necessarily indicate—it seems to me— a serious mind, however much we may be serious about those details. It is far more important to be serious about the total process of fear and also with what lies beyond fear; to enquire whether it is at all possible for us to be completely free, rid of fear. And that enquiry may be rather futile, because most of us still are caught in fear; but having discussed it during the several meetings that we have had here, I think we should go further and not keep on at that one issue.

As we were saying, a petty little mind, a narrow, shallow mind, is very concerned about details and is very serious about those details. But when presented with a greater issue—about which it has to be far more serious—then such

102

a mind hesitates because it doesn't see the full implication of what it is presented with. So this morning, if we may, we will go into the question of what the mind is; and in going into it, exploring it, we may perhaps come upon the beginning of all thought and perhaps something much deeper, which is love; we may find for ourselves what the meditative mind is.

In exploring this question of what the mind is, we see that the specialist—the neurologists, the various psychologists, and theoreticians, religious and intellectual, have defined it—more or less—as that which remembers, has the capacity to think, both reasonably and unreasonably; it functions not only technologically but more widely and is considered susceptible to certain intimations from something which is above, it contains both the conscious and the unconscious; it is the whole store-house of memory which is in the brain which is part of the mind; the mind cannot be separated from the body, and so on. It is important for each one of us here, to find out for ourselves what we mean by the mind—not according to these specialists, however capable, or according to the theologians, or to the religious people, but putting all that aside—to find out what the mind actually is. Then, after that, we could ask a further question—what is the origin of thought? Can one discover how thought begins? That discovery will reveal a still further depth, which we shall go into as we go along.

We should be able to find out for ourselves, what the mind is, the mind that is conscious, that thinks, that has the whole background of time; and the brain that reacts according to its conditioning, the brain that is the store-house of memory, which is part of the mind. And do we actually find out for ourselves, or are we merely finding what we have been told? I think this is important, this question as to whether you find merely what you have been told, which therefore is not your discovery, or whether you discover for yourself. If you find out for yourself what the mind is, from there you can proceed; but if you are accepting a theory, a communication about the mind, then you are dealing second-hand and what you find remains merely a theory, it has no value at all.

So, can one find out what the mind is? You know, to go into this question deeply one has to be in a state of meditation—not meditation according to some system or method, or with the desire to achieve a certain result, which is not meditation at all, but the meditation of a mind that is free to look, to observe, a mind that is extraordinarily quiet. And when you observe your own mind—that is, your whole consciousness—is there an observer which can examine? To examine that microphone, to see how it works, I must take it to pieces and see what is inside it. But in looking at this whole field of consciousness—which is the mind, which is the brain, the nerves, the whole store of memories and so on—is there in fact an entity which can look at it, examine it?—is there an entity separate from the thing it examines?—and if there is a separate entity then is that not invented by thought, and therefore part of the mind and not separate at all, therefore not able to find out what the mind is? How then is one to find out what the mind is, without that separate entity, the observer?

I want to know what my mind is, the mind that thinks, the brain that reacts, the thoughts that arise from memories, with motives, intimations, the self-centered pursuits, the ideas, beliefs, dogmas which are all within the field of this consciousness, which are all part of me. And I say to myself "I must look, I must find out what the origin of thought is, the beginning, I must find out what consciousness actually is." And when I say, "I must find out", is that "I" separate from the thing it is going to look at, examine, observe, therefore capable of looking objectively? If it is not, if that "I" who observes this totality of consciousness, which we call the mind, is not separate then how is it to find out, or be aware of, this total state which is called the mind?

I must be very clear on this point as to whether there is an observer which is separate from the mind for obviously if there is such an observer it is created by thought, it is

104

part of this consciousness and therefore it is not separate. Then how is the totality of the mind to be understood if there is not a separate entity who can say "I have examined" and "I have understood"? This demands a great deal of discipline—not self-imposed discipline, control, suppression—and the very act of looking, examining, itself brings its own discipline. I want to find out and to find out I am asking myself whether the observer is different from the mind that he observes. To ask that question, to find whether the observer is different, demands a great deal of discipline; not the discipline of conformity, because there is no pattern here. So the very asking of what the mind is and if there is a separate entity who observes that mind, is bringing about a discipline. This discipline is not conformity and is therefore freedom; freedom is related to discipline. Is this fairly clear? Not clear in the verbal sense but are you doing this with me? Are we going together? You can ask this question if you are free, if you have no opinions, no conclusions, no beliefs, and in the very asking of it there is austerity—you follow—you are putting away everything except that question which may open the door to enormous vision, enormous depths. So if the observer is part of the observed, if the mind which is consciousness has itself divided itself into the observer and the observed then it is a division that is erroneous; then what is the state that can be aware of this totality which we will call the mind? If the observer is the observed, if the entity that observes all this is part of the mind, then when I ask myself "What is the mind?" and the observer is not, what then is the state of the mind—what state discovers this, sees consciousness as it is, with its frontiers, with its limitations and so on? In asking this we are trying to find out what it is that is aware and which is obviously not separate, when there is no observer.

What is it to be aware? I am aware, sitting on this platform, of seeing different colors, the tent overhead, aware of the noise of that stream, the movement of one or two people, the silence—I am aware of this. In that awareness is there an observer who says "I am aware separately of that color and that color"? Because what we are going to question further, as we go along, is, if all consciousness is limitation—and all consciousness is limitation, in it there is no freedom whatsoever—then is it possible to go beyond that limitation, is it possible to experience that which is beyond the limitations of consciousness and if so, who is the entity who is going to experience? So I have to understand what is meant by awareness—to be aware. As I said, I am aware of all this and ask, "Am I aware as an observer separate from the thing observed or am I aware without the observer?" You know what love is—is there an observer who says "I love"? And if there is that observer, is that love? And when you say there is love, is there a complete absence of the observer? If the observer is not absent then that love becomes hate, jealousy, pain, anxiety, guilt,—you know all the rest of it—which is not love; it becomes merely desire and pleasure, which again is not love, which we went into previously.

It is very important to find out what we mean by being aware, being attentive. We have asked the question—what is the mind?—because we want to find out what is the beginning of all thought, and in that question we are asking—who is the entity who is going to find out?—who is going to receive the answer? If the entity is part of consciousness, or part of thought, then he is incapable of finding out; what can find out is only that state of awareness. In that state of awareness is there still an entity who is aware, who says "I must be aware", "I must practise awareness"? When you look at the blue sky this morning, those mountains and clouds, seeing the whole depth and height of the sky, when you are aware of all that, do you say—I am aware?—or is there only an awareness of all that, without the observer, though you see it with your eyes, with all the rest of it? That very seeing, without creating the observer, is to be totally aware. When one looks at that tree, is one aware of that tree without the observer? The observer is the entity who has gathered information about that tree and according to that information, image, symbol, he looks at that tree, such looking, with the observer, is not being totally aware of the actual tree. Is this somewhat clear?

That is—to bring it a little more directly—when you look at your wife or your husband, are you aware of the wife or the husband through the image which you have created about the wife or the husband?—or, are you directly aware of her or of him, actually, without the observer? This is an infinitely difficult thing to do—I can look at the sky, the clouds, the river and all the rest, because they do not intimately touch my feelings, my reactions, but when I have lived with somebody for a number of years I have created an image about that person, and that person has created an image about me. In these circumstances when we say we are aware, we generally mean the image becomes aware of itself in relation to the other image—which is part of awareness, but we have gone much farther than that. And we say that when there is this image there is a center which observes, there is a division and hence a conflict. Where there is conflict there is no awareness at all. To be free from conflict one has to become aware and do so without creating another center which is aware of the image that I have created about myself or about another. So, is there an awareness without the center, of this whole of consciousness, with its boundaries, its limitations, its content?—the very contents make the boundaries, the content of my consciousness, as the Hindu and all the stuff of education, experience.

So we are beginning to find out that thought has its origin, its beginning, in consciousness in which there is the division between the observer and the observed. Let's put it round the other way. How will you find out for yourself how thought, any thought, begins? Have you ever asked yourself that question? If you have, how will you find out? To find out anything, it doesn't matter what it is, your mind, the whole of consciousness—not a part of it—must be quiet, mustn't it? If I want to look at you, to see you very clearly, my mind must be very quiet, without all the prejudices, the chatters, the dialogues, the images, the pictures,—all that must be put aside to look at you. And then—because there is freedom and therefore quietness—in that state there can be observation. So can I—please follow my next question—can we, you and I, observe the beginning of thought? I can only observe the beginning of thought in silence—not when I begin to search, ask questions, wait for a reply—it is only then when my mind is completely quiet after having put that question—what is the beginning of thought?—when it is completely quiet right through my being, that I can begin, out of that silence, to see how thought takes shape. It is very important this question—because *if there is an awareness of the beginning of thought then there is no need to control thought.* As you know, we spend a great deal of time—not only in schools and colleges but as we grow older—controlling thought,—"this is good thought"—"this is bad thought", "this is a pleasant thought I must go with it", "it is an ugly thought I must suppress it"—and so on and so on—we control, suppress. There is a battle going on all the time between various thoughts, the mind is a battlefield, a field in which there is constant conflict, one thought against another thought, one desire against another desire, one pleasure dominating all other pleasures, and so on. But if there is an awareness of the beginning of thought, then there is no contradiction in thought.

Am I talking nonsense, or is there some kind of sense in it? I think there is a little sense in it, because you know, a life of conflict has no meaning whatever. The conflict with myself, or with a neighbor, or with ideas—I don't want any kind of conflict because every conflict is a tension, a distortion. A life of conflict wears itself out very quickly and one must find out if there is a way of living without one breath of conflict at any time in one's life. And I can only come upon that way of living when I begin to discover the beginning of thought. If the mind can discover without being aware of the center, then every thought is not a distraction. Every thought then has not its opposite, for there is only thought, not the opposing thought. Therefore it is an important question and one which has some sense in it and it is not quite nonsense.

One can see the beginning of thought only when there is silence, when mind has become silent, not through discipline, not through control, not through various forms of meditation and all the rest of that ugly business, but naturally. It is only in silence that I can discover anything; it is only then that the mind can find out and come upon this extraordinary discovery of something new. Such discovery is only out of silence and that silence cannot possibly be cultivated, it cannot be put together by thought; if it is put together by thought it is dead, it is stagnation. When thought puts anything together there is always conflict. So one comes upon the discovery of the beginning of thought because the mind is completely quiet, it doesn't matter what thought it is—thought. And if there is only thought it has no contradiction. Oh, you don't see this? There is only desire, but contradiction arises when there is the desire for this in opposition to that and when one begins to find out the beginning of desire then there is no contradiction. Contradiction implies conflict and one who wants to live without conflict has to understand this. To understand all this the mind must be silent and this silence is meditation. A mind that is extraordinarily alive and alert no longer stores up every discovery, and one comes upon something else—for a mind so greatly alert, alive, is a light to itself, without any experience.

Most of us crave experience, whether going to the moon or the experience of a little mind that seeks through drugs the state of a consciousness in which there are visions, heightened sensitivity and so on and so on; the mystical experience, the religious experience, the sexual experience, the experience of having a great deal of money, power, position, domination—you know— we all crave experience. And this because our own life is so shallow, so empty, so insufficient, and we think that without experiences the mind becomes dull, stupid, heavy. That's why we read book after book, we go to the museums, concerts, rituals, churches, football—every form of experience. But we never ask what is involved in this experiencing, or ask if there is anything new in experiencing. Every experience demands recognition, otherwise it is not an experience. If I don't recognize it as an experience involving something, it is not an experience. It is only when I recognize it that I call it an experience, but to recognize I must have already known. Through experience there can be no new thing at all. So one has discovered a fundamental truth, that a mind that is seeking, craving, searching for wider, deeper experience, such a mind is shallow because it lives always with its memories, with its recognitions, and what is remembered, recognized, is not the new. But there is no experiencing in silence and one asks how is it possible to act in this world if the mind is really quiet, silent? You understand? Is it possible to function, in this world, with this enormous sense of silence? One has a certain function, one has to do a certain thing, as a librarian, as a cook, as a technician, sit in an office and so on, which all demands accumulated information as knowledge, experience; and one asks, can my mind which has understood and is living in that state of silence function in these circumstances? When one puts that question, one separates silence from the action; it is therefore the wrong question. But when there is the silence one will function in the office. You know, it is like a drum that is highly tuned and you strike on it and it gives you the right note, but it is always empty, silent. It doesn't say—"I am silent"—"How am I to function in the office?"

So one discovers that all consciousness, both the hidden and the obvious, the secret and the surface, is part of this process of thinking. One can only be aware of the beginning of thought when there is silence, when there is no frontier to consciousness. All this demands a great deal of discipline in itself, not discipline for something, and if we have gone that far, we can then ask, what is love? You understand, it is necessary to enquire if love is within the field of consciousness, which is thought? I say "I love you, love my country, love my God, love my books, love my position"—you know—love. We see that word rather slackly yet rather intensely; when you say to somebody, "I
110

love you", what does that word mean? Religious people throughout the world have divided it into the profane and sacred and so on. Is love desire?—don't say "No" because for most of us it is, desire and pleasure, the pleasure that is derived through the senses, through sexual attachment and fulfilment, through my wife, my husband, my family as opposed to the other families, my country, my God, my King—you know all that stuff! We call that love, for which we kill others, in which there is jealousy, hatred. But is that love? In that love there is possession, domination, dependence, the seeking of satisfaction, pleasure, comfort, companionship—an escape from myself. It that love? Or does love lie beyond this turmoil of thought? If you say it does, then what will happen to my wife, my children, my family, they must have security—I must have security. If you put that question then you have never been outside that field of consciousness. When once you have been outside that field of consciousness you will never put that question, because then you will know what love is, love in which there is no thought, no tomorrow and therefore no time. But you will listen to this—pleased and probably mesmerized and enchanted—but to actually go beyond thought, beyond time—because time is thought and thought is sorrow—to go beyond is to be aware that there is a different dimension called love. From there one can act, one can be.

There arises another question—what is beauty? Is beauty in the object or in the eyes of the beholder?—or is beauty neither in the object nor the beholder but when the observer and the observed have been totally abandoned? This can only be when there is total austerity, but not the austerity of the priest with its harshness, with its sanctions, rules, obedience. Austerity means simplicity, not in ideas, clothes, in behavior or in food, but being totally simple, which is complete humility. Therefore there is never a climbing—therefore there is never an achievement—therefore there is no ladder to climb, there is only the first step and the first step is the everlasting step.

Without understanding beauty and love and meditation

—the real thing I mean—then life as it is, lived as it is, with its sorrow, pain, conflict, has very little meaning. You may take drugs to give it meaning, you may cling to your sexual appetites to give life a meaning, but dependence on any drug, on any thought, or any demand of pleasure, only brings about more conflict, more misery, more confusion.

Questioner: I just want to say, as you were talking about experience that since a few years I have had a tremendous craving to go up in a glider and I thought that would be really wonderful. Yesterday I had the chance to go up with a Swiss officer and glided for one hour—a most interesting experience—but when I came down it was just as if I had had that experience before. It was not necessary to go up.

KRISHNAMURTI: The questioner says he went up in a glider yesterday and he wanted to go up because he wanted to have a new experience.

Questioner: To do it myself.

KRISHNAMURTI: To do it yourself, another form of experience. And when he came down he found it was not an experience at all—he had already had it. Look Sir, why do you crave for experience, whether in a glider, or of sex, climbing mountains, taking drugs and getting psychedelic expansions and so on? Why do you crave for experiences? First ask that. And if you didn't have any experience, not one experience, what would happen to you? Is that possible? Now, we depend on experiences to keep us awake, experience is a form of challenge—without challenges do you know what would happen to all of us?—we would be asleep. If there was no political change, if there was no conflict within ourselves, if everything was as we wanted it to be and we were undisturbed, we would all be fast asleep. Challenges are necessary for most of us, different challenges and it is they that keep us awake. We depend on experiences—pleasant or painful—to keep us awake; every form of challenge we want, to help us keep awake. When
112

one realizes that this dependence on challenges and experiences only makes the mind more dull and that they do not really keep us awake—when one realizes that we have had, as we said the other day, thousands of wars and haven't learnt a thing, that we are willing to kill our neighbor tomorrow on the least provocation—then one asks, why do we want them and is it at all possible to keep awake without any challenge? This is the real question—you follow? I depend on a challenge, experience, hoping it will give me more excitement, more intensity, make my mind more sharp, but it does not. So I ask myself if it is possible to keep awake *totally*, not peripherally at a few points of my being, but totally awake, without any challenge, without any experience? That means, can I be a light to myself, not depending on any other light? That doesn't mean I am vain in not depending on any stimulation. Can I be a light that never goes out? To find that out I must go deeply within myself, I must know myself totally, completely, every corner of myself, there must be no secret corners, everything must be exposed. I must be aware of the total field of my own self, which is the consciousness of the individual and of society. It is only when the mind goes beyond this individual and social consciousness that there is a possibility of being a light to oneself which never goes out.

27th July 1967

10

WHAT IS IT EACH one of us is seeking in life? If we seriously put the question to ourselves, as to what it is, deeply, that we all want—I wonder what we would reply? Is the demand, the search, based on one's inclinations, guided by one's tendencies, or shaped by circumstances? If it is shaped by circumstances then it is merely a matter of making those conditions somewhat better, happier, more pleasant, more satisfactory. And if our demand is merely the dictate of tendency, according to our conditioning, to our culture, to our background, then it will naturally be enforced by our limited comprehension, our limited attention. If our demand, our deep search, is based on our inclination, then it is the search for greater and wider pleasure. Which of these three categories is it that guides, shapes or urges our search, our longings, our gropings? Apparently most of us are seeking something—greater pleasure, greater satisfaction, wider and deeper experiences—and there are those of us who are somewhat more serious and say we are seeking the truth. That word is one of the most dangerous words, for the search for truth demands not merely a casual intermittent drive, but rather a sustained, continuous looking, not in any particular direction, but a total comprehension of life. If we are seeking greater pleasure—which most of us are, and though there be nothing wrong with it—that greater pleasure brings with it greater pains and greater fears. And if there is merely a conditioned response, arising from tendency or circumstance, then it brings its own bondage, its own pains, its own sorrows. But if we are a little more cautious, hesitantly serious, then we shall be serious about everything in life. And one must be serious in life—not with regard to truth or pleasure or momentary satisfaction—but serious about everything that one touches, whether it is in the cooking of a delicious lunch or serious with regard to our relationship with another human being, or serious when one asserts to oneself that one is seeking something which is called "truth". I think one has to be extraordinarily, vitally, serious about everything in life—not about fragmentary parts of life—because each individual human being is responsible for all the misery, for the wars, for the hunger, for the brutalities and so on, for this enormous violence that exists in the world.

(For those of you, please, who are not really very interested, who merely came for curiosity, would they all get up and go now—it would be much simpler. If you are serious at all about anything then stay and pay as much or as little attention as you can.)

I feel very strongly that each one of us, being responsible for the chaos, misery and sorrow in the world, that each one of us as a human being must bring about a radical revolution in himself. Because each in himself is both the society and the individual, he is both violence and peace, he is this strange mixture of pleasure and hate and fear, aggressiveness, domination and gentleness; sometimes one predominates over the other and there is a great deal of unbalance in all of us.

We are responsible not only to the world but also responsible for ourselves, in what we do, what we think, how we act, how we feel. Merely to seek truth or pleasure without understanding this strange mixture, this strange contradiction of violence and gentleness, of affection and brutality, of jealousy, of greed, envy and anxiety, has very little meaning. Unless there is a radical transformation in the very foundation of ourselves, merely to seek great pleasure or to seek truth has very little meaning. Man has sought that thing we call truth, apparently, throughout historical times and before, an otherness which we call God, which we call the timeless state, a thing which is not measurable, which is not nameable. Man has always sought that because his life is very dull, there is always death, old age, there is so much pain, contradiction, conflict, a sense of utter boredom, a meaninglessness to life. We are caught in that and to escape from it—or because we have slightly understood this complex existence—we want to find something more, something that won't be destroyed by time, by thought, by any human corruption. And man has always sought that and not finding it he has cultivated faith—faith in a God, in a savior, faith in an idea. I do not know if you have noticed that faith invariably breeds violence. Do consider this. When I have faith in an idea, in a concept, I want to protect that idea, I want to protect that concept, that symbol; that symbol, that idea, that ideology is a projection of myself, I am identified with it and I want to protect it at any price. And when I defend something I must be violent. And more and more, as one observes, faith has no place anymore; nobody believes in anything anymore— thank God. Either one becomes cynical and bitter, or one invents a philosophy which will be satisfactory intellectually—but the central problem is not resolved.

The central problem is really: how is one to bring about a fundamental mutation in this complex, unhappy world of confusion, not only outside but inside?—a world of contradiction, a world of such anxiety. Then, when there is a mutation, one can go further, if one wants. But without that radical, fundamental change every effort to go beyond that has no meaning. The search for truth and the question

116

as to whether there is a God or not, whether there is a timeless dimension, will be answered—not by another, not by a priest, not by a savior—by nobody but yourself and you will be able to answer that question for yourself only when there is this mutation that can and must take place in every human being. That is what we are interested in and concerned with in all these talks. We are concerned not only as to how to bring about a change objectively in this miserable world outside of us, but also in ourselves. Most of us are so unbalanced, most of us are so violent, greedy, and are hurt so easily when anything goes against us, that it seems to me the fundamental issue is—what can a human being, such as you and I, living in this world, do? If you seriously put that question to yourself I wonder what you would answer—is there anything to be done at all? You know, we are asking a very serious question. As human beings, you and I, what can we do, not only to change the world but ourselves—what can we do? Will somebody tell us? People have told us; the priests who are supposed to understand these things better than laymen like us, they have told us and that hasn't led us very far. We have the most sophisticated human beings, even they have not led us very far. We cannot depend on anybody, there is no guide, there is no teacher, there is no authority, there is only oneself and one's relationship with another and the world, there is nothing else. When one realizes that, faces that, either it brings great despair from which comes cynicism, bitterness and all the rest of it, or in facing it, one realizes that one is totally responsible for oneself and for the world, nobody else; when one faces that, all self-pity goes. Most of us thrive on self-pity, blaming others, and this occupation doesn't bring clarity.

What you and I can do, to live in this world sanely, healthily, logically, rationally, but also inwardly to have great balance, to live without any conflict, without any hate, without any violence, seems to me to be a question which each of us has to answer for himself.

This morning if we can travel together, not along a verbal line, not along intellectual concepts, but by putting

117

aside all those things, take a journey and find a state of mind which is never in conflict, and which therefore has no element of domination or servility. To find such a state of mind we must journey together and that means you will have to give a great deal of attention, not concentration, for there is a difference between attention and concentration. When you concentrate what actually takes place? watch it in yourself. When you concentrate on something, when you focus your thought, force it to be concentrated on something, there is a process of defense, there is the building of a wall within which the mind can concentrate upon something. Concentration is an exclusive process whereas attention is not. "To attend" means to give complete attention, not a fragmentary or partial attention, that is, listen to the aeroplane, or the train going by, listen to the talk, see, hear and feel everything completely without any frontier, then in that state of attention we could journey together very far and very deeply.

We are asking what one can do, as a human being living in the world and in himself, being both violent and gentle, both full of antagonism and hate, or with an occasional burst of joy, what can one do to bring about a revolution in oneself. Now this requires attention. (At this moment there is a failure of the public address system and an attempt is made to remedy this while the talk proceeds.) There is a distraction going on here and my tendency is to observe what is taking place and yet to resist that tendency because I want to talk; so there is a contradiction—you're following all this?—so there is a conflict and in that state the mind cannot function clearly. The mechanical thing has gone wrong, it has to be put right, at the same time I have to talk clearly and to think without any contradiction; mere concentration won't bring that about. But whereas if there is attention, attention to what is going on, not being distracted by it and yet with that attention a listening to what is being said, then there is no contradiction. It is in that state of attention that we can look at ourselves and the more we know about ourselves the more deeply can the mind penetrate within itself and go beyond all the intellectual and verbal structures and symbols so that it is not caught in its own imagination, in its own illusion, in its own desires.

So first, you and I must know ourselves *completely*, so that there are no hidden corners, no secret untrodden recesses of the mind. Either you do this, step by step—please follow this very carefully—step by step through analysis, through examination, through opening every layer of one's consciousness, which means you take time—that is to say I'm angry, I am jealous, I am envious, and to understand why, the motive of it, to uncover, to unroll the vast and complex me, that will take time—either one does that, or there is a different way altogether. Please understand this very clearly. I can analyze myself, I can look at myself, if I want to, without any illusion, without any perversion, I can look at myself very clearly as I can look at myself in the mirror, and by looking at myself I begin to analyze, to go into the cause of every movement, of thought, every feeling, enquire into every motive, and that will take a lot of time. It will take days, months, years, and in this process there is always distortion going on because there are other influences, other pressures, other strains. So that when I admit time in this process of understanding myself, I must allow for every form of distortion. And 'myself' is such a complex, deep entity —moving—living—struggling—wanting—denying, and I have to watch every movement to understand the whole of it. Either I do that or do what is generally done, that is, I identify myself with something greater, with the nation, with the state, with the family, or with an idea, as of the Savior, of Buddha; I identify myself with that, a projection from myself, an idea of what I want to be, or what I should be, and in that there is conformity to that pattern and hence more struggle. That is what man has done throughout ages, he has either gone inwardly, through introspection and analysis, or he has identified himself with something, or he has lived in a state of total negation, hoping that something will happen. Man has done all this and even more complex things and he has taken drugs. It

119

is not only the modern world that is taking drugs, for the taking of drugs existed in China three or four thousand years ago, as it existed in India, and all to escape from the monotony of life, from the terrible boredom and the meaningless existence of going to the office every day, to have sex, to have children, to be in constant battle with oneself. Man has needed an escape of some kind, whether it is the escape of the football field or the escape of a church, they are exactly the same. So, if all that is not the way, because all that implies time and the sowing of more seeds of violence, antagonism, if you really understand that, then you put it away completely. You see that that is not the way. It's like a man who wants to go south but who has taken a path that leads north, suddenly when he realizes that is not the way then he turns his back to the north. It is the same when one realizes that all those attempts that human beings have made throughout time are not the way—it doesn't matter who says to the contrary —then you can look at yourself in quite a different way, you can look at yourself without time.

There is this total complex thing called "me" with its antagonism, fears, hopes, aspirations, ambitions, greed, the whole thing that is me; can I look at it so completely and instantly that I understand the whole thing? After all, what is truth?—the seeing of truth, the feeling of what truth is, with its beauty, with its love—how does one see that? You can only see truth when the mind is not fragmented, when you see the totality. When you see the totality of yourself, all of it, not just the fragments here and there, but the totality of your being, that is the truth and you understand the whole complex.

Can one look at oneself so completely, so attentively that the whole of oneself is revealed in an instant? Most of us cannot do this because we have never approached the problem so seriously, we have never looked at ourselves, never. We blame others, we explain things away, or we are frightened to look at ourselves and so on, and we never look at ourselves as we are. You can only look totally when you give your whole attention. In such attention there is no fear, for when you're giving your mind, your body, your nerves, your eyes, your ears, everything, to look, there is no room for fear, there is no room for contradiction, there is no conflict. When you have looked at yourself so deeply, then you can go even deeper. When using the word "deeper" we are not being comparative. We think in comparisons—depth and shallowness, happiness and unhappiness—we are always measuring. When I say, "I must go deeply, or deeper in myself" the word "deeper" is a comparative word. Now, are there such states as the shallow and the deep—in oneself? When I say, "my mind is shallow, petty, narrow, limited"—how do I know it is petty, narrow, limited? It is because I've compared my mind with your mind which is much more bright, has more capacity, is more intelligent, aware, and so on. Then I say, in comparison, "my mind is shallow, my mind is petty" but can I know my pettiness without comparison? Do I know that I am hungry now because I was hungry yesterday or, do I know that I am hungry now without comparison with the hunger I knew yesterday? So when we use the word "deeper" we are not thinking in comparative terms, we are not comparing.

A mind that is always comparing, always measuring, will always engender illusion. If I am measuring myself against you, who are clever, more intelligent, I am struggling to be like you and I am denying myself as I am, and I am creating an illusion. So when I have understood that comparisons in any form only lead to greater illusion and greater misery, that when I analyze myself, or when I identify myself with something greater, whether it be the state, a savior, an ideology, when I understand that all such comparative thinking leads to greater conformity and therefore greater conflict, then I put it completely away. Then my mind is no longer seeking, no longer groping, searching, asking, questioning, demanding, waiting—which does not mean that my mind is satisfied with things as they are—then my mind has no illusion or imagination. Such a mind can move in a totally different dimension. The dimension in which we live, the life of everyday, the pain,

121

pleasure, and fear that has conditioned the mind, that has limited the nature of the mind, all that is completely gone. Then there is enjoyment, which is something entirely different from pleasure. Pleasure is brought into being by thought, as thought brings into being fear. But enjoyment, the real joy, the feeling of great bliss, is not of thought. Then the mind functions in a dimension in which there is no conflict, there is no sense of "otherness", no sense of duality.

Verbally one can go only so far; what lies beyond cannot be put into words for words are not the thing. You understand—the actual tree is not the word "tree", the word is different from the fact. Up to now we can describe, explain, but the words or the explanations cannot open the door. What will open the door is daily awareness and attention. Awareness, without any choice, of what is going on within, of how you speak, what you say, how you walk, what you think; being daily aware of it. It's like cleaning a room to keep it in order, but keeping the room in order is of no importance; it is important in one sense and totally unimportant in another. There must be order in the room but the order will not open the window. What will open the window, the door, is not your volition, is not your desire. You cannot possibly invite the "other". All that you can do is to keep the room in order; which is to be virtuous, but not the virtuousness or morality of any society for what it will bring, but to be virtuous for itself, to be sane, rational, orderly. Then perhaps, if you're lucky, the window will open and the breezes will come in—and they may not. It depends on the state of your mind, and that state of mind can only be understood by yourself, watching it yet never trying to shape it, which means watching it without any choice. Out of this choiceless awareness perhaps the door will open and you will know what that dimension is in which there is no conflict, no time, something which can never be put into words.

Do you want to ask any questions on what we have been talking about this morning?

Questioner: Sir, imagination—what is that?

KRISHNAMURTI: What is imagination—don't you know? Do you want an explanation of that? You all know what imagination is, the fairy stories, the imaginative paintings, the invention of heaven and hell, the invention of gods, the imagination in memory, of that beauty which you saw yesterday evening in the cloud and so on. We live on myths and phantasies. A mind that is capable of inventing, imagining and projecting itself into various forms of visions, is such a silly mind.

Questioner: Sir, how is it possible to make any kind of art if we do not have any imagination; that would be impossible?

KRISHNAMURTI: What place has art for mind which is a religious mind?—not the phoney religious mind that belongs to some church, or that believes in some doctrine or in some philosophy, such a mind is not a religious mind at all—but to a mind that is living in a totally different dimension, to that mind, has art any meaning at all? Why is it that we depend so much on music, poetry—why? Is it a form of escape, a stimulation? You paint a picture and I look at it, I criticize it and say, "how beautiful" or "how ugly". Or, if you become famous, it fetches a great price. But if you are directly in contact with nature, the hills, the clouds, the rivers, the trees, the birds, if you watch and are with the movement of a bird on the wing, the beauty of every movement in the sky, in the hills, in the shadows, or the beauty in the face of another, do you think you will want to go to any museum, to look at any picture? Is it perhaps, because you do not know how to look at all the things about you, that you go to the museum to look, or you take mescaline, marijuana, drugs to stimulate you, so that you can see better? One has to question everything that man has accepted as valuable, as necessary. You may have questioned the political tyrants, the dictators of reli-

123

gion, but you have never questioned the authority of a Picasso or of a great musician. We accept, and in that acceptance we grow weary and we want more pictures, more non-objective art and painting, and so on. But if we knew how to look at the face of a passer-by, at a flower by the roadside, a cloud of an evening, to look with complete attention and therefore with complete joy and love—then all these other things would have very little meaning.

Questioner: The state of complete attention is, in other words, a state without conflict; so is not to understand the state of being without conflict a presupposition of a state without conflict?

KRISHNAMURTI: It's a vicious circle, isn't it? I live in conflict, my mind is in constant conflict, whatever it does is a strain and it's caught in that and the speaker says—"in that state you will never understand anything", it is only when you are attentive that you will understand this whole process. But, to be attentive is not possible because my whole mind is in a state of conflict, so it becomes a vicious circle. Or, are you, the speaker, aware that you have created this vicious circle and that you have left us with the circle and nothing else? So what is one to do?

Being caught in a vicious circle, the speaker not telling us what to do, doesn't solve the problem. Now if you will kindly follow what I am saying, I am sure we will understand each other. First of all I realize that my mind is in conflict, whatever it does, whatever movement it makes it is still within the limits of that conflict. Whatever it does, whether it aspires, whether it desires, whether it imitates, whether it is conforming, suppressing, sublimating, taking drugs to expand it—whatever it does, it does in a state of conflict. If I have understood that, understood it not merely in the verbal sense but by actually seeing it as clearly as I see that microphone, without any distortion, then what takes place? If I see something very clearly, as when I see something very dangerous, like a precipice or a dangerous animal—what happens? All movement, for a moment, stops, there is no thought. In the same way if I really see what thought does, thought comes to an end. Whatever thought does it breeds misery, sorrow, conflict, and when thought realizes that, it will come to an end by itself, the vicious circle is broken; thought, which means time, has come to an end.

Questioner: Is this stillness, this awareness, synonymous with meditation?

KRISHNAMURTI: That word "meditation" is a very loaded word and in Asia it is given a particular meaning. There are different schools of meditation, different methods or systems of meditation, various systems which will produce attention. There is a system which says "watch the movement of your front toe", "pay attention to it, work and watch it, watch it" and so on. Meditation as control, following an idea, looking on an image endlessly, taking a phrase and going into it, listening to the word Om or Amen or some other word, listening to the sound of it, following the sound, and so on. In all those forms of meditation there is implied an activity of thought, an activity of imitation, a movement of conformity to an established order. To the speaker those are not meditation at all. Meditation is something entirely different. Meditation is to be aware of thought, of feeling, never to correct it, never to say it is right or wrong, never to justify it, but just to watch it and move with it. In that watching and moving with that thought, with that feeling, you begin to understand and to be aware of the whole nature of thought and feeling. Out of this awareness comes silence, not simulated, not controlled, not put together by thought, for silence put together by thought is stagnant, is dead. Silence comes when thought has understood its own beginning, the nature of itself, how all thought is never free but always old. To see all this, to see the movement of every thought,

125

to understand it, to be aware of it, is to come to that silence which is meditation, in which the "observer" never is.

30th July 1967

dialogues at saanen

1

WE ARE GOING to talk things over together for six days. I think we ought to be clear what these so-called discussions are. They are a dialogue, a form of conversing seriously together about problems, going into them not only analytically, carefully, but also seeing the whole structure of each problem: not merely the details of it, but its whole form and content. As this is a conversation, a dialogue between you and the speaker, we ought to be vulnerable; that is, not have any defense, any resistance, but be willing to expose ourselves completely not only to the problem, but to what is involved in the problem, giving our whole attention to it. So this dialogue, this conversation is not an intellectual amusement, a mere exchange of arguments—one opinion against another, or one formula against another formula, or one experience against various other experiences. Rather it is to look into the very problem itself and not merely be concerned with how to be rid of it, how to go beyond it; nor how to have a concept or a formula, which we hope will solve all problems. So we are not dealing with ideas, we are not concerned with an idea which is yours, or that of the speaker. What we are concerned with is the fact, with what is—what actually is! Then if you and the speaker both accept that we are starting with what actually is—not what you think about it or what you think it should be—then our relationship in this dialogue will be entirely different; it won't be a one-sided affair. It will be worthwhile to be vulnerable to everything that is said, not rejecting anything; so that one begins to be very sensitive, alert to the problem itself. If this is somewhat clear and I hope we shall clarify it as we go along during these six days meeting here every morning, then we can with profit go into the various problems that we have.

So what shall we talk about?

Questioner (1): I don't quite understand the phrase, "a light unto yourself"; and also having no challenge related to experience.

Questioner (2): I wonder what is the right use of our faculties? You said during the last conference that even art and science as well as financial or political activities may be an escape. What can we do with our faculties which won't be an escape from actual life itself?

Questioner (3): To understand violence one has to understand also the fact of loneliness with its hopes and fears—could we go into this?

Questioner (4): Could we discuss the problem of having a goal in life, an aim and purpose and not being conditioned by it?

Questioner (5): What is right action?

Questioner (6): Could you go into the question of identification with regard to feeding the ego?

KRISHNAMURTI: Now which of these questions shall we take?

Questioner (7): What is thinking?

Questioner (8): Could we have a purpose in life without being conditioned?

Questioner (9): My question is also about motive—this is a school which is being started in Santa Barbara and I have a problem—about the motivation of being completely passive. I don't do anything; I just respond to the immediate situation—but there is the question of one's motive.

KRISHNAMURTI: When we discuss one subject very closely, intimately, in detail, perhaps we shall be able to touch all these problems. So which of these problems that have been raised shall we take up and go into completely?

Questioner (10): Discussing the purpose of life will involve all other questions.

Questioner (11): Maybe we can discuss questions, Sir. What are fundamental questions?

KRISHNAMURTI: That's what I was going to ask. What is a fundamental question? Are we asking a fundamental question? I'm not saying you're not; I'm just asking. Will these questions we have raised this morning reveal the ways of our thinking, will they reveal in detail the issues which we want to understand? Or are we asking peripheral questions, questions that are rather superficial? I'm not saying that they are but I want to find out what is a fundamental question. For instance, a fundamental question (it appears to me—I may be mistaken) is this question of violence, the problem of vulnerability—being vulnerable—because defense implies violence. Any form of resistance is violence. And if we are going to discuss violence, is it a problem to you or is it merely an idea? You see there is so much

131

violence in the world today and I want to understand it. Is the violence out there, or here? If it is here, then what is my question? Do I want to solve the violence out there—expressing itself in racial riots in America, violence in Vietnam, every form of violence that exists outside—or are we questioning violence in itself, as it is in me, which expresses itself outwardly? Therefore, in questioning this violence, I'm vulnerable to discover the truth of it. But if I'm merely examining the violence outside me, it becomes of academic interest. So when we put all these questions, are we relating them to ourselves, or to an objective fact outside of us? (I hope I'm making myself clear on this point.)

Questioner: Sir, instead of asking the question "what is violence?", the fundamental question is "why am I violent?"

KRISHNAMURTI: It comes to the same thing, Sir. Why am I violent and do I know the nature of violence, do I know what is implied in that violence? Sir, we must be clear how we converse about this. Are we exchanging ideas, opinions, or are we conversing together so that we can penetrate more and more deeply into this fact of violence, which is in us? Therefore, if we are discussing violence, we must be vulnerable to this fact and not resist it: not say "I am not vulnerable", "I am above all violence" (which would be absurd) nor say, "I'm only concerned with the improvement of the world and stopping violence out there". So, we are conversing together over the problem of violence, not as an idea, but as a fact that exists in a human being. And the human being is me!—not the Vietnamese, the American, the Russian, the Egyptian, the Israelite—it is me, here, as a human being. And to go into this question I must be *completely* vulnerable, open! I must expose myself to myself; not necessarily expose myself to you—because you might not be interested—but I must be in a state of mind which demands that I see this thing right to the end, and therefore be vulerable right through: at no point do I stop and say, I won't go any further. If we could so discuss,
132

go into this, it would be really extraordinary. So shall we take violence? Yes? (Approval) Right.

Why do you want to take it? Why do you want to enter into that subject?

Questioner (1): Because we are violent, I am violent.

KRISHNAMURTI: You say, "I want to go into it because I am violent."

Questioner (2): I want to take violence, go into it, because I'm a violent human being.

KRISHNAMURTI: I have experienced violence as anger, violence in my sexual demand, violence as hatred creating enmity, violence as jealousy, and so on—I have experienced it, I have known it. And I say to myself, I want to understand this whole problem, not one aspect of it, not one fragment of it—as war or as hate—but aggression in man (which exists in animals of which we are part). I am a human being, I am violent. Now, is that what you feel?—as a human being, not driven by circumstances to be violent—you understand?

There are two schools of thought; one says "violence is innate in man"; "violence is part of his nature, he's born with it, it is his structure." The other says "violence is the result of the social or cultural structure in which he lives." Right? That is, human beings are innately violent, or they are violent because society has made them so. We are not discussing which school you belong to. What is important is that we are violent; and is it possible to go beyond it? That is the whole question; not whether it is innate or is the result of the social structure in which we live. Now let's proceed. I am violent—right? Now what do you mean by that word "violent"?

Questioner: Hostility.

KRISHNAMURTI: I know, Sir, aggressiveness. But how do you

know you are violent? What does that word mean to you?—not according to the dictionary—but how do you know when you are violent?

Questioner: I am angry, violent, when I can't get what I want. . . .

KRISHNAMURTI: Sir, just a minute, let's begin very simply. Anger; we all know anger or irritation. Would you call anger violence? Go slowly, Sir. You would call it violence, wouldn't you? Now, there is righteous anger and unrighteous anger. When my wife or sister is attacked I'm righteously angry; when my property is taken away from me I'm righteously angry. Wait, wait! I don't say you are that way—you may have no property. I'm just saying there is righteous anger and unrighteous anger. When my country is attacked, my God, my ideas, my principles, my habits, I am angry. I take drugs and if anybody says it's wrong I am very annoyed. So, when you say "anger" is there righteous anger, ever? No, Sir, please—go into this very carefully—or is there only anger? There is not good influence and bad influence, but only influence. That means, when you are influenced by somebody which doesn't suit me, I call that "evil influence." There is only anger; not "righteous" or "unrighteous" anger—right? We have experienced that. You tread on my toe and I get angry. You say something to me which I don't like and I get angry; or, you take away the money, the substance on which I have lived, I get angry; or, my wife runs away with you and I get jealous—that jealousy is righteous, because she is my property. (Laughter) No, no, Sirs, please, don't brush it away by laughing. That is justified legally, morally, in the Church, religiously, and so on. That is justified. To kill for my country is also justified, legally. So, when we are talking about anger, which is a part of violence, do we look at anger in terms of righteous and unrighteous anger, or do I see anger?—not in terms according to my inclination. Now, how do I look at anger?

Questioner (1): It is something to do with the "I."
134

Questioner (2): It's me.

KRISHNAMURTI: But how do you look at it, how do you feel about it?

Questioner: I want to protect the me and what belongs to me (or I think it belongs to me). . . .

KRISHNAMURTI: Therefore, it is righteous.

Questioner: It is never righteous, but it is.

KRISHNAMURTI: The moment you protect it, it becomes righteous. The moment I protect an idea, the family, the country, the belief, the dogma, the thing that I demand, that I hold—as long as I protect it, that very protection indicates anger. I don't know if you see this?

Questioner: My violence is energy to get something.

KRISHNAMURTI: Yes Sir. Violence is part of this drive to acquire. But for the moment, Sir, we are trying to go into this question of anger which is part of violence. How do I regard anger? How do you?

Questioner: I am part of anger.

KRISHNAMURTI: No, no, Don't reduce it to "I am anger." How do you look at it, how do you feel about it?

Questioner: Sir, can I look at anger when I'm not angry? otherwise it's part of memory. . . .

KRISHNAMURTI: The questioner says, "at the present moment I am not angry, when I look at anger it is a memory which I have had and I look at that." That's good enough. Of course at the present moment your property is not threatened, your wife is not taken away—you're not angry.

But wait a minute, you'll get angry presently if I tackle (laughter), if I approach something which you hold on to?—an idea, a belief, a dogma, as your country, as your God, as your Queen, King, whatever it is. If I say to you, if you take drugs, "how childish it is," you will be annoyed. So, how do you consider anger? Can you look at anger without any explanation, any justification, any sense of protection? Can you look at anger as though it was something by itself?—I'm putting it wrongly. Are you aware of anger the moment after?—or at the moment you are angry?

Questioner: Certainly, I think, when I'm angry, Sir.

KRISHNAMURTI: When you are angry, at that moment, are you aware you are angry, or when the thing is over? "I am angry." The adrenal glands are working and everything: anger! Am I aware at that moment, or, a moment after?

Questioner: The moment after! I can't feel it in the moment if I can't stop it.

KRISHNAMURTI: No, please, please look at it, do let's consider before we answer it. We are discussing anger a part of this enormous complex thing called violence; how do I look at that anger? Do I look at it with my eyes which say, "you are right, you are justified in being angry" or, do I look at that anger condemning it?

Questioner: If I can notice that I'm angry at the very moment. . . .

KRISHNAMURTI: No, Madame, that's not the question we are asking. We are asking, "how do I regard anger"? Do look at it. You have been angry, how do you look at it, how do you consider it? Do you justify it or do you condemn it?

Questioner: I condemn it—it depends on my state of mind—.

136

KRISHNAMURTI: No, no Madam, it is not your state of mind. Do you condemn it and justify it?

Questioner: Sometimes I don't. . . .

KRISHNAMURTI: Look Sir. Do you condemn war? Do you? or do you justify war?

Questioner: Not all war.

KRISHNAMURTI: Madame, do consider it, please don't answer so quickly. Do you condemn homosexuality? Yes? No? Why? You see, you haven't considered these problems, you are just reacting. Here is an enormous problem: anger; how do you look at it, how do you consider it? Can you look at it completely objectively?—which means you neither justify it, nor condemn it? Can you do that?

Questioner: Can we consider anger by considering what it is not to be angry?

KRISHNAMURTI: No, Sir, no Sir. I am angry, Sir, do please follow this for two minutes. I am angry. I either justify it or I say, how stupid of me to be angry.

Questioner: Why not be angry?

KRISHNAMURTI: Be angry! All right! But you are not meeting my point. If you're angry and you like it, be angry. If you enjoy it, if you feel that it is righteous, if you feel it gives you a great deal of satisfaction—you can't kick your wife but you kick somebody else, so it gives you a tremendous feeling of fulfilment.

Questioner: I didn't mean that, Sir; I am angry. . . .

KRISHNAMURTI: Ah, you're angry. All right. Now please, Sir, do stick to one thing, I beg of you. I am angry. Being angry how do I regard it?

137

Questioner: At the moment of anger I do not regard it in any way.

KRISHNAMURTI: Right Sir. That's understood. At the moment of anger, you are in it, you can't look at it. But the moment after how do you consider it? Righteous or unrighteous, justified, or do you say, it's terrible to be angry? What is your position?

Questioner: One is bewildered.

KRISHNAMURTI: Oh, no.

Questioner: Sir, I think the first reaction is not as you suggest—one wonders about it and then you fall into temptation—you start to analyze it and look at the problem and its indications.

KRISHNAMURTI: So, you either condemn it or justify it.

Questioner: Of course! You wonder about it.

KRISHNAMURTI: Wait. You wonder about it, which means you want to know why it has come, what are the motives and what is the reason of your questioning that anger. Go slowly, Sir. Go into it slowly. What is the motive of your examination of that anger?

Questioner: Because it's an uncomfortable feeling.

KRISHNAMURTI: That's it. You don't like it.

Questioner: No.

KRISHNAMURTI: Therefore you condemn it.

Questioner: Analysis is condemnation.

KRISHNAMURTI: Of course it is.
138

Questioner: And that brings up a problem then.

KRISHNAMURTI: Wait, wait, Sir, don't bring another problem. Go step by step into it. So your attitude towards anger is that of condemnation, you cannot look at anger objectively, which means being vulnerable to it.

Questioner: Yes, that's the problem.

KRISHNAMURTI: Wait, keep to that, we'll develop it as we go along. You condemn it and I justify it. I say, "perfectly right." I have a right to be angry because you trod on my toe, or you said something insulting to me. So, I justify it and you condemn it. Neither of us can look at anger objectively. That's all my point.

Questioner: Right.

KRISHNAMURTI: Now, how will you understand anger if you do not look at it objectively, which means, neither condemning it nor justifying it?

Questioner: But that means going with it.

KRISHNAMURTI: Ah, wait. First—don't go with it or against it, just look at what is involved in it. Can I look at you if I'm antagonistic to you? I can't. Or, if you say, what a marvellous chap you are, I can't either. So, I must look at you with a certain care in which neither of these two things are involved. Now in the same way can I look at anger, neither justifying it nor condemning it? Which means I am vulnerable to that problem—you understand Sir?—in that there is no protection, I don't resist it, I am watching this extraordinary phenomenon called anger without any reaction to it. You understand Sir?

Questioner: I hear those words but I don't really see what you're driving at.

KRISHNAMURTI: I'm not driving at anything. I am just saying it is impossible to understand anger if I justify it or condemn it, that's all. Wait. If you say "obviously," then you will look at anger hereafter objectively.

Questioner: (In French) Is it possible to consider anger without any motive? I always justify or condemn.

KRISHNAMURTI: That's what we are saying, Sir. Do please give thought to this thing. I am angry, either I justify it or condemn it and therefore I never understand it—right? Can we put away this feeling of justification or condemnation when we look at anger?

Questioner: Anger is not objective and therefore I can't look at anger objectively.

KRISHNAMURTI: Can I look at my anger inwardly without identifying with it, which means justifying it or condemning it, which means resisting it? I don't see how you're going to go into the deeper issue when you don't understand this very simple fact. To comprehend something I must look at it completely dispassionately—right?

Questioner: It is impossible when we're angry.

KRISHNAMURTI: At the moment of anger you're lost, but the moment after, or when preparing yourself not to be angry in the future.

Questioner: Anger is an excess of vitality.

KRISHNAMURTI: Why do you limit vitality to anger only? You see you don't go into this.

Questioner: Sir, I don't think we know what it means to look at something dispassionately.

KRISHNAMURTI: We're going to go into it, Sir. If I cannot look at myself dispassionately, I can't go beyond that.

Questioner: *I deal with the pleasant feeling, the opposite of the anger. . . .*

KRISHNAMURTI: No, but I examine it too; I don't just examine what I don't like, I examine everything.

Questioner: *How can you look at a passionate state dispassionately?*

KRISHNAMURTI: You can look at passion without identifying yourself with it, or condemning it. But, Sir, you haven't even taken the first step—to look. I want to understand myself, *myself* being a very complex entity—a living thing, not a dead thing! I want to understand that. How do I look at myself?—I have to learn to look at myself. To look at a child I mustn't condemn him or adore him, I must have the eyes to look at him with care, with affection; not the affection which says, "he's my baby" but to look at him. In the same way I have to look at myself; and part of myself is this violence; and anger is of this violence. I say, now I am angry, I have known anger—can I look at it?

Questioner: *Essentially, however, is the mind not like the "I," it cannot see itself?*

KRISHNAMURTI: Sir, when you say, that the mind cannot look at itself you have stopped all enquiry, you have blocked yourself.

Questioner: *(In French) One knows anger—one can't do anything about it.*

KRISHNAMURTI: That is, one can't do anything about anger, one just accepts it. All right, accept it!

Questioner: *I dare not see anger, I'm afraid of it. Is not anger part of fear?*

141

KRISHNAMURTI: Of course, but that's not the problem. Now, let's begin all over again.

Questioner: Can't I look with a sense of curiosity.

KRISHNAMURTI: Look Madame, let's find out. Have you looked at a tree or a cloud without condemning it or accepting it? Passing it by have you stopped and looked at a tree or a cloud without any movement of thought? Have you? Well apparently you haven't.

Questioner: (In French) Could we consider fear?

KRISHNAMURTI: Wait, wait. Sir, look. I want to understand the beauty, the movement of the tree, I want to look at it. It's outside me so I can look at it, it doesn't interfere with my thoughts, with my wife, with my husband, with my property—it is there! So I can look at it quite objectively, can't I? Now, how do I look at that tree? Do I look at it with all my thought going, chattering, or, when I do look at that tree, my mind is quiet, because that tree is extraordinarily beautiful, I look at it. What do you do?

Questioner: Nothing, but looking.

KRISHNAMURTI: Which means what?

Questioner: Being there, watching.

KRISHNAMURTI: In that watching there is neither condemnation nor justification, is there? You just look—right? Like a flower, you look at it. Which means, no interference of thought—right? Now, to look at anger is much more difficult, isn't it, because it is subjective, it affects you. If you have not been able to look at a tree so dispassionately, how can you look at yourself, who are part of violence? And that's what we are trying to do. Here I am. I am violent as a human being. I don't know whether I've inherited it or the society around me has produced this violence in me. I

142

am brown, black and you're all white—and you don't like brown, black, purple people—so you dislike me and so I get angry. And here I am violent; I'm not concerned whether I've inherited it or society has given it to me, what I am concerned with is whether it is at all possible, first of all, to be free of it. I'm really interested—you understand? It means everything to me to be free of violence. It's more important to me than sex, food, position—this thing is corrupting me and I want to understand it, I want to be beyond it. And to be beyond it I can't suppress it, I can't deny it, I can't say, "it's part of me." I don't want it! And, I have to understand it, I have to look at it, I have to study it, I have to go into it. I must become very intimate with it and I can't become intimate with it if I condemn it or justify it—right? But we do condemn it, we do justify it. Therefore, I'm saying—stop, for the time being, condemning it or justifying it.

Questioner: How can I be objective to my condemnation and my justification?

KRISHNAMURTI: Sir, you can be objective to your condemnation or justification when you realize that they interfere when you are looking at anger. When I'm concerned with anger and trying to understand it, justification and condemnation interfere with that study of it, therefore I have to put it away.

Questioner: I don't.

KRISHNAMURTI: You don't because to you the study of anger is not important; to me it is enormously important. Therefore as it is so important, these minor things don't matter. Sir, I want to understand affection, love. I must give my whole being to it, I must study it, I must be familiar with it, I must know every corner of it. And because of my tremendous serious intention and interest in that, everything else becomes secondary. So, when you are studying anger, you're either studying it as a curiosity or

143

you're studying it because you want to understand this thing that is destroying you—destroying the world. I want to understand it, I want to be free of it, I want to be above and beyond it. Therefore, I'm not interested in condemning or justifying it—it has no value. It reduces it to a personal, petty little affair. Right? Can we proceed? Sir, are you really interested in understanding anger—anger which is part of violence, part of hate?

Questioner: It means we have to have energy to look at it.

KRISHNAMURTI: Of course, but you're dissipating that energy when you're condemning it or justifying it.

Questioner: (In French) If I don't see very clearly and deeply that one must consider this problem of violence and anger, if by listening to you about it I become serious, am I not merely being stimulated by you to be interested?

KRISHNAMURTI: You are right. The questioner says, "am I being stimulated by you, the speaker, to be interested in anger or am I really interested in it apart from any stimulation?" You see how little we have advanced? We have spent an hour over something very simple. That is, I can only look at anger when I'm really passionately interested to find out if it is possible to go beyond it. But apparently you're not interested in it.

Questioner: In all the questions during the last hour, it appears that none of us is as serious as you are. That makes it rather hopeless.

KRISHNAMURTI: It's up to you, Sirs! You mean to say you are not interested in war?

Questioner: . . . . not the way you are.

KRISHNAMURTI: Not the way I am—aren't you?—don't you want to stop wars, don't you want to stop violence? Of
144

course you say you do. But how much vitality, what energy, what will you give to it?

Questioner: Would you discuss meditation in relation to anger?

KRISHNAMURTI: We are doing that, Sir. We are really meditating about anger.

Questioner: Maybe we should discuss communication. Isn't that what you meant when you said. . . .

KRISHNAMURTI: Of course, of course. So, could we discuss or talk over for a while what communication means. You may be tremendously interested to resolve this problem of violence, but I'm not. I'm casual about the whole thing. How do we communicate with each other? I say to you, "I love you," and you say "yes, it's a nice day, isn't it?" and pass by. (No, you laugh. It doesn't mean a thing to you!) When I say, "I love you," you must listen, you must stop, you must see if I really mean it. Then you can reject me or whatever you like. But first you must stop, there must be communication, there must be a sense of together understanding the thing. There is the question of violence, and to you it is not important whether your children are killed, whether your sons go to the army, are trained, bullied, butchered—you don't care! You say "all right, let's talk about it."

May we ask a question? Why is it that you don't care? You understand? Your daughters are going to get married or it is your son who is going to be called to the army. In America that's going on—they're dodging conscription, the draft. Our sons are being sent to Vietnam to be shot to pieces—aren't you interested? My God! And if that doesn't interest you, what does? Keeping your money? Having a good time? Taking drugs?

Questioner: I believe it is an assumption to say that we are not interested.

145

KRISHNAMURTI: I didn't say that. I very carefully didn't assume anything. I said, if you're not interested in violence, which means your children being destroyed, what are you interested in? Are you interested in some abstraction?

Questioner: *But we are interested in violence.*

KRISHNAMURTI: All right. If you are interested then listen with your heart and mind to find out! Don't sit back and say, well tell us all about it. The speaker points out that to look at anger, you don't look at it with eyes that condemn or justify, put that away. And you can't put those two away if this anger isn't a burning problem. I don't know if you have seen a picture in a newspaper, an incident in New Delhi? A man with a long stick is hitting another who is Chinese. Have you seen that picture? A crowd is standing around him, people with hands in their pockets—and these are the Indians who have been told for centuries not to hurt. You understand Sir? When you look at that picture you realize what human beings are. And I am part of it, a human being. And I say to myself—how am I who am responsible for all this (I feel responsible, you understand? I feel responsible, it isn't just a set of words) and I say to myself, I can only do something if I am beyond anger, beyond violence, beyond nationality. That feeling that I must understand brings tremendous vitality, energy and passion to find out. So, first I have to learn how to look at anger; I have to learn how to look at my wife, at my husband, at my children; I have to learn how to listen to the politician, I have to learn now—you understand, Sir? I have to learn why I am not objective, why I condemn or justify, I have to learn about it. I can't say, well it's part of my nature. I must know, so I have to tackle the question of learning. What do you think is the state of mind that learns?

Questioner: *Silence.*

KRISHNAMURTI: Silence? Do you learn Italian when you're
146

silent? or French, or German?—a language which you don't know. You can't be silent. You buy the book, you read it, all the verbs, the irregular verbs and go into it. In the same way we have to learn. You don't assume that first I must be silent and then learn. Here is something that you don't know. You don't know how to look at anger, therefore you have to learn, and to learn you have to study why you justify, why you condemn. You condemn and justify because it is part of your social structure, part of your inheritance. It's the easiest thing to do: to condemn or justify. You are German—out! Or you are a Negro—you cannot associate! That's the easiest thing to do! But study means care; you must love the language that you are studying.

Questioner: When I'm angry I see that physics and chemistry are going on inside me.

KRISHNAMURTI: Of course. Chemical changes are taking place when you're angry, but knowing chemical changes are taking place doesn't stop you from anger.

Questioner: One has to discover something much more fundamental. . . .

KRISHNAMURTI: Of course, Sir. But to discover something much more fundamental one must have the capacity to go deeply. If one has a blunt instrument, one can't go deeply. Now what we are doing is to sharpen the instrument, which is the mind. The mind has been made dull by justifying and condemning; if I see that I can only penetrate very deeply when my mind is as sharp as a needle, a diamond that can penetrate very deeply, then I demand such a mind, not just casually sit back and say, how am I to get it, but I want it as I want my next meal. And to have that I must see what makes the mind dull, stupid; what makes the mind dull is this scene of invulnerability which has built walls round itself; part of the wall is

147

the condemnation and justification. If the mind can be rid of that, then I can look, study, penetrate.

Questioner: (In French) I feel myself responsible for violence, but I'm surprised that many people here don't seem to feel it.

KRISHNAMURTI: What am I to do, Sir? I don't care whether they take it seriously or not. I take it seriously; that's enough. I am not my brother's keeper. To me, as a human being, I feel this very strongly, and that's all; what can I do? I will see that in myself I am not violent. I can't tell you or somebody else: don't be violent. It has no meaning, unless you yourself want it.

2nd August 1967

2

Yesterday we were saying that we would go to the very end of this problem of violence. To do that we have to be quite serious and put our mind and heart into it so that when we do analyze the nature of violence we are not only examining it intellectually, verbally, but also seeing violence in ourselves—as aggression, anger, hate, enmity and so on. And becoming aware of that violence in oneself, to see if it is at all possible to go above and beyond it and never come back to it again, never in any form be violent in oneself. Most of us take a pleasure in violence, in disliking somebody, hating a particular race or a group of people, having antagonistic feelings about others. There is a certain pleasure in this, which I think most of us are aware of. But I don't think we realize that there is a far greater state of mind in which all violence of any sort has come to an end. In that there is far more joy (I dislike to use the word enjoyment) than in the mere pleasure of violence with its conflicts, with its hatred and fears. So if we are at all serious we should by discussing, by the exchange of ideas, thoughts, feelings, we should discover whether it is at all

149

possible totally to end every form of violence. I think it is possible and yet to live in this world, in this monstrous brutal world of violence.

We took a part of this violence, which is anger, and we were trying to find out how to meet it without suppressing it, sublimating it, or accepting it. We said that it is quite an art to look at anger without any justification or condemnation. To look at ourselves without accepting or denying, to see ourselves exactly as we are, is quite a difficult thing to do and therefore one has to learn how to look. If one knows how to look at violence outwardly in society—wars, riots, the nationalistic antagonisms, the class conflicts—then perhaps we can observe violence in ourselves: sexual, ambition, aggression, the violence of defending oneself. Then perhaps we shall be able to go beyond it.

So can we, in dialogue, in conversation, seriously go into this matter? Unless you are one hundred per cent serious it has no value. When one is hungry one is very serious. Here is a complex problem which has existed for centuries upon centuries. Man has been violent; religions have tried to tame him throughout the world and none of them have succeeded. Perhaps Buddhism and at one time Hinduism tried to create, to bring about a human being who was not at all violent. But if we are going to discuss this question we must, it seems to me, be really very serious about it. Because it will lead us into quite a different domain, into quite a different way of life. And I do not know if you want to go that far, or merely play with it for amusement, for entertainment, intellectually. So shall we go on with what we were discussing yesterday about violence?

Questioner: There seems to be contradiction in the words used. You speak of violence and of being aware of it without any movement of the mind searching for an explanation. Now on the contrary you say, let's analyze violence!

KRISHNAMURTI: We said, we have not only to analyze the structure and nature of violence (which is in ourselves) but also in the very process of analyzing we shall perhaps come upon that state of mind which is totally aware of the whole problem. You follow, Sir, what I mean? Most of us don't even know how to analyze. I do not think through analysis anything is going to be achieved. I cannot get rid of my violence through analysis. I should probably justify it, or modify it slightly, live a little more quietly with a little more affection; but analysis, whether with the professional or through oneself will not lead anywhere. When one realizes that this process of analysis does not lead anywhere, discovers for oneself that this analytical process has no end and has no meaning, then perhaps one will have a mind that begins totally to be aware of the whole problem.

Questioner: Yet you talk of not analyzing.

KRISHNAMURTI: If I do not know how to analyze, how to look, I cannot come upon the other. I cannot have this total perception if I don't know how to look. My mind has been trained for generations to analyze; it is extremely arduous to realize that analysis in any form doesn't lead anywhere. But I must know how to analyze, otherwise I cannot come upon the other. This means, in the very process of analysis my mind becomes extraordinarily sharp, and it is that quality of sharpness, attention, seriousness that will give a total perception. You see, we are so eager to get the total, to see the whole thing in one glance. But we haven't the eyes to look. It is only possible to have that clarity if I can see the detail and then jump.

Questioner (1): Yesterday you did not translate my last question (from French), so will you allow me to repeat it in English? I am very conscious of my share of responsibility in this disintegrating world. The rich have even more responsibility for this disintegration. There are rich people who have listened to you, some of them for forty years; they are still more responsible. The presence in this tent of such persons represents a static force in contradiction to

151

what you have been saying for forty years. There is an urgent need for each one of us to understand what you are saying, because of this disintegration. But whose role should it be to denounce vigorously the sabotage which this static force constitutes?

Questioner (2): He is trying to say that the primal root of aggression is a static force that uses you as a scapegoat to escape. . . . because nothing ever happens, never.

Questioner (3): I also have a point. This disintegration is coming very quickly now and perhaps one day we shall not be able to hear you in this tent.

KRISHNAMURTI: The problem, putting it in a very few sentences is this, isn't it? The rich, apparently from what you say, are using the speaker as a drug and therefore the whole thing becomes static. Right? Therefore this disintegration is more rapid. That's the problem, the question.

I don't know why we are concerned with the rich or the poor, nor who is disintegrating or not disintegrating; whether somebody is using the speaker as a drug, to stimulate himself and therefore remains static, or those who take actual LSD and remain static. They have an activity but it's still an activity which is a disintegrating process. Now I don't see, as we said yesterday, why we are concerned with another. We are concerned first with what we are—you and I. Leave the others alone! Whether rich or poor, Communist or Socialist, Hindu or Buddhist—leave them alone! You and I are responsible! You who are listening and I who am talking. I am responsible. And whether you use me, the speaker, for your own amusement, enjoyment, as a drug—that's your affair, it's your misery. Whereas what we are talking about is something entirely different. We are not talking about the individual or the society; we are talking about a human being who is beyond the individual and society, how to bring about such a human being—that's what we are concerned with. Not whether next year there will be a tent or not, whether I speak or don't speak. (Interruption) No, no, Sir. What are we concerned with? Primarily, essentially with bringing about a radical revolution in the human being—whether he is rich or poor—anybody! And if we lose our energy in saying, "well, why haven't the people who have listened to you for forty years changed?"—it's their affair! Sir, look. I believe the speaker has talked for more than forty years. It's my tragedy, not yours. And it would be a tragedy to the speaker if he was expecting something out of it, expecting people to change, to bring about a different society, a different way of life. If I was expecting it I would be disappointed, I would be hurt, I would feel I had not done what I started out to do. It doesn't affect me at all! Whether you change or don't change, it's up to you. The blue sky, the hills, the flowers, the birds don't exist for you; they exist for themselves. So let's proceed, Sir, to discuss this matter.

We are violent human beings. To say, "you have not changed, why haven't you?" is a form of violence. That's the communist way, which is to brainwash people to their particular ideology. We are not doing that here; it doesn't mean a thing to me to convince you of *anything*. It's your life, not my life; the way you live is your affair. And if you want to live with great happiness, great bliss, with a great sense of ecstasy, we'll walk together, we'll communicate with each other. If you don't, you don't, and what am I to do? Human beings are violent and is it possible for that violence to be totally eradicated? That is the only question we are concerned with, not whether the rich or poor are better; all that has no meaning.

Now is it possible for me and for you to end violence in yourselves? Which means, I must find out for myself what kind of violence there is in me. Is it defensive violence to defend myself? I defend myself through my nationality, through the religion I belong to, through an ideology, whether it is Communist or Catholic or Buddhist, or whatever it is. The very process of defending and resisting is a form of violence. When a nation says, I defend myself only, such a concept obviously means I am prepared to

153

fight. So there is no such thing as defense and offense, because both contain in themselves, violence. That's one form of violence. Then there is a form of violence which is anger, in which is involved hate, jealousy, aggressive acquisitiveness, the demand to dominate, to possess; all those are forms of violence. Or do you call violence merely killing another? Is it not violence when you use a sharp word against another? Is it not also violence when you make a gesture to brush away a person, or when you obey, because there's fear? So violence isn't merely killing another—in the name of God, in the name of society, in the name of the country—this organized butchery. Violence is also much more subtle, much deeper, and we are enquiring into the very depth of violence. If one is not subtle enough, clear enough to follow to the very end the root of violence, which is both in the conscious as well as in the so-called deeper layers of consciousness, I don't see how you can ever be free of violence. After all, why shouldn't one be violent? We take it for granted that we should not be violent. I don't know why. You've had in Europe two dreadful wars, with all the brutality, the exterminations of the concentration camps, the butchery, and yet you haven't changed. You're still Germans, Austrians, Russians, Catholics and all the rest of it. So you have accepted that as the way of life—haven't you? Obviously Sirs. And can you voluntarily, sanely (not neurotically) put away that? Psychologically begin with that and see where it will lead you. Can one do that? My friend up there says it cannot be done.

Questioner: (in French) Is it not a question of the emotions?—one has bouts of anger.

KRISHNAMURTI: Certainly it is related to emotion. Which is what, Sir? Look, you hit me for whatever reason (I've insulted you). There is an emotion—anger—but that anger is sustained by thought. Thought gives to that feeling a continuity. I hate you hereafter because you have hit me. I want to hit you back, I'm watching, waiting for an opportunity to hurt you, which is all the process of thinking.

Questioner: (in French) It is not rather the relationship of the emotions?

KRISHNAMURTI: That's only a part of it. Take this whole thing—emotion, thought, the power to retain, which is memory; from that memory, my conditioned responses, I act. I am a Catholic, a Communist, I have been conditioned that way and if anybody attacks that, questions that, I get annoyed, angry, which is an emotional response according to my conditioning. We're saying, can one go to the very root of violence and be free of it? Otherwise we are not human beings, we shall live everlastingly in a battle with each other. If that is the way you want—which is apparently what human beings want—then carry on. But if you say there might be a different way of living, there might be a different process of responding to life, then we can discuss, then we shall be able to communicate with each other. But if you say, well I'm sorry, violence can never end, then you and I have no means of communication, you have blocked yourself.

Questioner (1): That is to say, I must not say there is no end to violence, for I don't know.

Questioner (2): In discussing violence we soon arrive at the central problem, which is how to look without the interference of thought. I think all problems are fragmentations, but there is a central problem. So why are you speaking about violence and not the central problem, how to look—at anything?

KRISHNAMURTI: We are conditioned to violence and in violence. Now, how do I look at that violence? I am conditioned and can I look at that violence, at that conditioning without any distortion? The problem is quite complex. My mind is distorted, because it is conditioned.

155

Right? My mind has been for centuries shaped in a particular culture, a particular society, through time, experience, knowledge, memory—it is conditioned, shaped, held within a narrow pattern of the me. Can such a mind become aware of its own conditioning? And when it becomes aware of its own conditioning, who is aware of the conditioning? So, first are you and I aware of our conditioning? Then we can take the next step. Am I aware of my conditioning as a Hindu, living abroad, living in a culture which is totally foreign to the Indian culture, brought up along certain lines as a Messiah, and all the rest of it? (I'm doing it as a mirror in which you're looking.) Can you become aware of your conditioning, can you become conscious of it? Look, Sir, as a Hindu, a Brahmin, brought up in a particular culture, from childhood it was said, "don't kill, don't hurt a fly, don't say a word against another, don't be aggressive"—that has conditioned the mind from childhood. And if it is merely a conditioned response which says "don't be violent" then it is another form of violence. You follow? It's like a Catholic saying there is a Savior, there is sin, and only this Savior can save. That's a conditioned response, it has no meaning whatsoever. But this mind which from childhood has been told, "don't kill, don't hurt, because next life you'll pay for it, therefore behave, be gentle, be kind," can that mind which has been shaped day after day become aware of its own conditioning—and then move further?—which we would if you would go along with the speaker, not follow him as disciples and all that tommy rot, but go along with him. Can you become aware of your conditioning—one's conditioning? Can you?

Questioner: *To be without conditioning, isn't that a kind of death?*

KRISHNAMURTI: I don't know what it means. How do you know it means death? It might mean a much more extraordinary way of living. Why do you say to be out of conditioning means death? We don't know.

156

Questioner: A kind of death.

KRISHNAMURTI: But, Sir, I don't know. I won't say it is death. First, my question is—can I, can you, become aware of your conditioning?

Questioner: (In French) One cannot, it is an essential part of living.

KRISHNAMURTI: Sir, look. We are conditioned by the climate, by the food we eat, by the newspapers we read, by the company we keep; we are conditioned by the wife, by the husband, by the job, by techniques, by everyday influences and experiences. We are conditioned! Now, can I become aware of that conditioning: just one conditioning?

Questioner: (In French) One can begin with this certitude.

KRISHNAMURTI: Whether it is pleasurable conditioning or unpleasant conditioning, are you aware of your conditioning?

Questioner: One conditioning interacts on another.

KRISHNAMURTI: Yes, Sir, I know they are all related to each other, but I am saying, begin with one conditioning, as an Englishman, as a Frenchman, as a Catholic, or if you are inclined towards Communism, or peculiar sexual abberations—just one conditioning!

Questioner: I am aware of some of my conditioning, but nothing happens.

KRISHNAMURTI: Why should anything happen? Nothing happens because you don't feel that you are caught like a prisoner within four walls of a conditioning. A prisoner within four walls says, "I am in prison, I want to get out of it!"

Questioner: Sir, it is possible to be aware of one's conditioning, the state one is in. I know it.

KRISHNAMURTI: Look Sir, please, take one conditioning and become aware of it; see how seriously you are aware of this conditioning and whether you enjoy it, or you want to break through all conditioning?

Questioner: I think, Sir, that I was aware to a certain extent of my conditioning as a Jew during the Middle East crisis, and I recall this gave me a mixture of great pleasure and great discomfort.

KRISHNAMURTI: Yes, Sir. When one is aware of one's conditioning, as a Jew, as a Hindu, as a Negro—whatever it is—then in it there is not only great pleasure, but also as you say great discomfort. Now, does this conditioning bring a sense of imprisonment or not? Or, do you say, well the pleasure outweighs the discomfort and therefore it's all right. You follow what I mean? Or, do you say, it isn't good enough.

Questioner: Something in me says, it isn't good enough.

KRISHNAMURTI: All right, something in you says it isn't good enough and how far are you going to go into this question and break it? That is the whole issue. One knows very well one is conditioned—I've had money, leisure, I can think more, or think less, or go to nightclubs, enjoy myself and all the rest of it; or I'm conditioned because I'm a poor man and I want more money, more comfort, more this and that. Now, when I become aware of this, how far do I want to go into it and break through it? Because most of us are aware of our conditioning. If one is at all sensitive, thoughtful, serious, earnest, one is aware of one's conditioning, and also what it results in, what its dangers are. If I am aware as a Hindu opposed to a Chinaman,

158

then I am at strife with the Chinese; but if I realize to what depth it leads one—to what anxiety, brutality, hate—I want to break through it. So, how far are you willing to go into this question of conditioning as violence?

Questioner: How far dare any man go in being aware of his conditioning without coming to a precipice?

KRISHNAMURTI: Then when you come to a precipice you know how dangerous your conditioning is. But without coming upon that precipice you play with your conditioning. So, are you willing to push the awareness of your conditioning until you come to that precipice—when you've got to act! Or, are you merely playing with your conditioning from a safe distance?

Questioner: Most people are not conscious of their conditioning, but are satisfied as they are. They don't see another mode of living. But if we are deeply hurt by circumstances of life as a consequence of our conditioning, our eyes are opened. But it's a rare event.

KRISHNAMURTI: If you are aware of your conditioning, how far will you go, how deeply, until you come to the point when you've got to act?

Questioner: And then—

KRISHNAMURTI: Not, "and then," not "and then." That's a supposition.

Questioner: Why don't I, when seeing part of my conditioning, see a precipice? Why?

KRISHNAMURTI: Wait, shall we discuss that? That is, you are aware of your own conditioning, but it never comes to the point where you've got to act as you do when you're

159

confronted with a danger, as a precipice. Now, why? Is it that one is lazy?

Questioner: Yes.

KRISHNAMURTI: Just wait, Sir. Don't answer so quickly. Is it that one is lazy, laziness being lack of energy? Will you lack energy when it is really dangerous?

Questioner: If we don't suffer because of our conditioning we are satisfied. For instance, I feel security in my country.

KRISHNAMURTI: First of all, I am aware of my conditioning and I don't see what the results of that conditioning are. That's one point. I am a nationalist and I don't see where that nationalistic spirit leads to, so I like it, I enjoy it, it gives me pleasure. But if I saw the danger of it—wars—I would then act. Right? Now, I either don't see the danger of it, or, I don't want to see the danger of it because being a nationalist is a great pleasure; and to see the danger of it I must have energy to go to the very end of it. Why is it that I have no energy? Please stick to that one point.

Questioner: It's also dangerous to stand alone, without a group, without being attached to something.

KRISHNAMURTI: Of course, Sir. To stand alone, to be alone is the most dangerous thing, we all want to be with somebody; but that's a separate point.

Questioner: If you really see—with all the consequences— but we don't really see.

KRISHNAMURTI: Wait, wait, that's my point. If we saw that nationalism is danger to our own security—leading to war, to self-destruction—if you saw the danger you would act, wouldn't you? So the question is, you don't see. Now,
160

please just stick to that one thing. What do we mean by *seeing*? That is, I can see rationally through thought, analysis, examination that the nationalistic spirit does lead to war. In that analysis there is no emotional content, it is purely an intellectual dissection. When there is an emotional quality in this analysis—because it threatens me—then I become vital. So, the question is, what do we mean by seeing? Do I see detail by detail and put them all together and then say, well I've seen and so act? Or do I see this nationalistic conditioning and the result immediately? You follow Sir? It is only when I see something immediately that I see the danger—not as a process of thought, analysis. When you see a precipice there is an immediate action. So, *seeing is acting!* Right? Not, I see and then create an idea and from that idea act. That's what we are doing. And hence there is a conflict between the idea and action, and therefore that conflict takes away your energy.

Questioner: (In French) I've understood that, but. . . .

KRISHNAMURTI: First, let me swallow (laughter), let me assimilate what has been said, which is very difficult Sir. The speaker says, that seeing is acting. That is, I see a serpent and there is *immediate action*. I see a precipice and there is action. (It's very complex, this thing. Go slowly.) Or, I see, then have an idea about what I have seen, a conclusion, and from that conclusion I act. So there is a gap between seeing and acting.

Questioner: It is easy to see the danger of nationalism, but it is more difficult to see the danger of money.

KRISHNAMURTI: Money is equally dangerous. I see conditioning as an idea. I have an idea about my conditioning, the idea being I must be free of my conditioning. With that idea I'm aware of my conditioning. So, what sees is

161

not actual seeing with attention, but an idea sees another idea. Right? And therefore there is no action. So, let's go into it again. How do I see my conditioning? That's the first question. How do I see it? How am I aware of it? Are you aware of it as you are aware that it is raining? Raining is a fact that is actually taking place, it's not an idea. It is actually raining at this moment. You may not like it, you may be saying, how am I going to get my car out; but the fact is it is raining. In that there is no idea. Now, when you see your conditioning do you see it as a fact, as you see it is raining?

Questioner: The difference in the two states is, that in one the impression has an overriding urgency (as one sees the precipice or hears this rain); but the crisis of the moment is almost invariably diluted by a contrasting stream of impressions that come in and disturb one's attention. So. . . .

KRISHNAMURTI: Look, Sir. When you see a danger there is immediate action. There is immediate action because you have known danger before, you have been told "be careful of snakes," or you have been bitten by a snake, or you have heard that snakes are poisonous and you know somebody who has been bitten and died. So there is that memory which, when you see a snake, responds immediately. So that response to the danger is already old; you know already how dangerous a snake is. That isn't a direct response; it's a cultivated response. Time is involved in that response. Right? When you were a child you were told "be careful," and you remember it when you see a snake. That seeing is a cultivated, quick response. Now move to the other, which is this. You are aware of your conditioning, but you also have the memory that it is pleasurable, that it is right, that you cannot live in this world without being conditioned and so on. Again you have a response of time, of memory. But we are talking of a response which is not of time at all, which is not a cultivated response.

162

Questioner (1): (In French) One must efface memory.

Questioner (2): The difficulty is, the two seeings, "I am conditioned," and "it is raining," are wrongly identified as alike.

KRISHNAMURTI: Of course, Sir. Look, Sir, can I see without the movement of thought? The movement of thought is memory, because all thought is the response of memory, therefore it is always old.

Questioner: And the problem comes with memory.

KRISHNAMURTI: When I see a danger, I act. In that action, which seems spontaneous, instantaneous memory is involved; therefore it's not spontaneous, not immediate—it's already calculated. Then there is seeing my conditioning and responding to that conditioning according to my memory—pleasure, pain, satisfaction and so on. And we say, such a form of seeing does not produce an immediate action, which is not of memory. And it is only when you can look without the movement of thought—which is memory—it is only then that you break through your conditioning. Wait, wait, Look. It's a tremendously complex thing, Sir, it isn't just agreeing or disagreeing, this is a tremendous problem. Can I look at my friend, my wife, my husband without the image? The image which I have created about her and she has created about me, these two images have relationships—which are memories—and can I look at my wife, husband, without the image? No, don't answer me, find out! Can I look at my conditioning without the image? Therefore can I look at my conditioning without another conditioning? Otherwise, one conditioning looking at another conditioning only creates conflict—which is a waste of energy. So, is it possible to look at you, or you to look at me, without the image you have about me or I have about you? Which means, can I look at everything in life as though it was new?

163

Questioner: That implies. . . .

KRISHNAMURTI: It doesn't imply anything! Do it.

Questioner: It implies a dying, Sir.

KRISHNAMURTI: I don't know what it implies, do it!

Questioner: That means abandoning yourself. . . .

KRISHNAMURTI: You see you're theorizing. But can I look at you as though I'm meeting you for the first time, though I've known you for forty years? Can I look at that sky, that friend, that face, as though I was looking at it for the first time? If you cannot do it then you don't understand this whole business of conditioning. I may be aware of my conditioning, but that's not the problem, that's a very small affair. There's a much deeper issue involved in this conditioning, because we can never look without it, never! Therefore we are always living in the past with the dead. And that's a terrible thing to realize—you understand Sir? to realize I am looking at life from a dead past. To realize it! To feel it!

Questioner: But we are conditioned since birth. You can only see without it if you don't allow time to enter, which means being spontaneously aware.

KRISHNAMURTI: Sir, I said so! I said, from the moment you are born until the moment you die you are conditioned. Therefore if you like it, remain in it.

Questioner: But it is so. . . .

KRISHNAMURTI: We said so, we all agree.

Questioner: We must be continuously aware. . . .

KRISHNAMURTI: Please Madame, don't reduce everything to "continuously aware." See one thing very clearly, which is, that I can never see anything except through my conditioned eyes. That is it! To realize that is a tremendous shock to me. You understand? It's a shock to realize that I'm a dead human being. No?

Questioner: And can I see sometimes. . . .

KRISHNAMURTI: Do you realize that you are a dead human being when you say that you see with conditioning, therefore you are looking at life with the past? That's all. Can one realize that?

Questioner: How do you know that human beings are conditioned, since you don't involve yourself? I mean, you tell me. . . .

KRISHNAMURTI: No Sir, I don't tell you anything.

Questioner: But you're talking. . . .

KRISHNAMURTI: I am talking because we said at the beginning of these discussions that it is a dialogue, a conversation between two people who are serious, who want to go into this question of violence, of conditioning. And we see that we look at life with our conditioning, life being my relationship to my wife, to my husband, to my neighbor, to society. We are looking at everything with closed eyes. That's all. And how is it possible to open my eye? Nobody can do it. Religions have tried to tear my eyes apart by believing, by dogma, by rituals, and all the rest of it. And the Communists say, you can never be unconditioned, that's part of life, always live in prison only decorate the prison more and more. But a man who says "such a way of living is not freedom," must find a way out of this; and to find a way out is to become aware of your own conditioning and discover that you look at your own conditioning through conditioned eyes. Find out whether you can live in that state! Do you know, Sirs, I have watched snakes—

several of them round me—poisonous cobras—in India—
many of them. And you know what happens to you? You're
terribly awake! You're watching everything! Your nerves,
your eyes, your ears are listening to every movement! And
that's the way to live with yourself—without going mad.

3rd August 1967

3

IF WE MAY, we'll continue with what we were talking about yesterday, which was violence. I think we should be clear what these dialogues, these conversations are meant for. For the time being it seems to me that it is so utterly futile to be concerned with another: to be concerned with the rich or with the poor. Our concern is with a transformation that is necessary within oneself. Because, as we said the other day, we are the result of the society which each one of us has created: in the state in which we live there is no difference between society externally and psychologically, inwardly. We are trying to understand the structure and the nature of the psyche of each one of us and we are concerned with bringing about a radical transformation—to go beyond and above this conflict, this violence. Violence, not only externally, but also inwardly—the conflict, the contradiction (which breeds aggression, hatred, antagonism)—we are trying to understand what this violence is, what this aggression is, and whether it is at all possible to go beyond it. And that's what we are going to go into during these remaining dialogues.

We were discussing yesterday the question of "seeing": how we look at things—the things outside of us and the things in us—how we look at them. When we see a danger of any kind we respond to it according to the memory that has been cultivated. When we see a precipice or a dangerous animal we act immediately, but in that immediate action there is the whole cultivation of memory which responds instantly—which one can observe. Also, when we observe ourselves, we look with our conditioned mind, which is again cultivated; and we are saying: as long as this conditioned memory responds in any form there is no understanding, there is no seeing. There is action only when seeing is acting: the seeing which is not conditioned. There is nothing very difficult about understanding this; but the difficulty arises when we have to apply it, act. We act according to our conditioning. That again is fairly obvious. If I'm a Communist, a Socialist, a Catholic, a Hindu, a follower of Zen (or whatever it is) I act according to my background, according to my conditioning. That conditioning may be the result of centuries, or the result of a few days. Hence, the action is according to an idea which has cultivated. That again is fairly clear—right?

Now, as long as there is a separation between idea and action, there must be contradiction and therefore there must be conflict, and this conflict is violence—isn't it? I have an ideology—Catholic, Communist, whatever it is—and according to that ideology, ideal, or tradition, I act; I approximate the action to the ideal and hence there is a contradiction and in this contradiction there is conflict. The very nature of violence is this contradiction—right? I am violent and there is also in me a sense of kindliness, gentleness, so there is a contradiction. This contradiction contributes to greater violence. And we are asking ourselves whether it is at all possible to act without conditioning, and hence act without contradiction, effort and violence. Please, this requires a great deal of enquiry, understanding; it mustn't just be accepted. Because all of us have ideals. To me, to the speaker, every form of ideal or ideology, whether it be Communist, Catholic, Hindu or whatever it is, is idiotic, it has no sense; because it prevents not only seeing and therefore acting, but it prevents the understanding of the total structure of violence. Are we going with each other so far? What do you say, Sirs? This is not a talk by me, this is a dialogue between us, a conversation.

Questioner: What is it that sees and acts at the same time?

KRISHNAMURTI: You know, the varieties of action, most of our actions are based on a memory, an idea, a concept, a formula: "what should be," "what has been" and "what must be," and according to that we act—don't we? No? (Are you sure we are understanding each other?) And we say, as long as there is a division between an action and an ideal there is contradiction; because the ideal is always old. Ideals are always the result of the past projected into the future and therefore all ideals are always the old; but, action is always in the present, it is an active present: to act. Now the important thing is to understand this, not only verbally, but actually see how each one of us acts and see what is implied in this action (that is, the idea and the action, and the conflict involved in it, which is a contradiction) and to ask ourselves the question: is it possible to act without the idea? Right?

Questioner: . . . . Is it action you speak about, or also the thinking, inside.

KRISHNAMURTI: Speak in Italian.

Questioner: (In Italian) When we see danger there is rapid action and in that rapid action memory is involved; is what you are talking about an action which is instantaneous, yet also a response of memory?

169

KRISHNAMURTI: Look Sir, we'll take another example, let's look at it quite differently. I ask you a question with which you are very familiar. I ask you, what's your name, where do you live, and your response is immediate. Why? Because you are familiar with your name, you are familiar with where you live, so the response is immediate; but in that immediacy there is a time interval also. It isn't instantaneous, there is a time interval. In that time interval the mind has acted extraordinarily quickly and given the answer. Right? If you ask a more complicated question, you have a time interval between the question and the answer. There, the memory is operating, searching, asking, looking; then after having found the answer you reply. And if the question is very, very complicated you take a long time— perhaps days, weeks, months. All that implies an activity within the field of memory, whether it is instantaneous, or whether there is a lag of time; all that implies the activity of memory and memory is always conditioned. Now we're asking: in that activity of memory, which is always conditioned and hence must always create contradiction, hence conflict (and conflict implies violence) is there an action which is not conditioned? So we are asking whether there is an action—please follow this—an action in which the time interval does not exist? You understand? So we have to enquire much more deeply into this question of what is thinking and what is consciousness.

Questioner: Sir, I don't see why that time interval always has to be just the response of memory. After all, we cannot stop what limited intelligence we do have—such as an intelligent appraisal when faced with a situation.

KRISHNAMURTI: Wait, follow it! The operation of that intelligence has produced violence also. Now, to be free of that violence we have to bring about a different quality of intelligence. Right? And that's what we are seeking, what we are asking ourselves. The intelligence that we have cultivated—which is the result of time and memory—that intelligence is within the limitations of thought.

170

Questioner: But this action without any ideal may also bring conflict.

KRISHNAMURTI: Of course, Sir, of course.

Questioner: A well known example might be a little child, newly born, he sees for the first time the fire, he is attracted by the light of the fire, but then he touches the fire and he burns himself. . . .

KRISHNAMURTI: We all know this, Sir. What is the point?

Questioner: But he has acted without any ideas.

KRISHNAMURTI: And then he has an idea afterwards, and according to that idea he acts. Of course, we know this Sir. That's what we are all doing, all the time.

Questioner: But if we act according to an idea it doesn't always bring a conflict, it gives perhaps a rational event or something like that. . . . you never know. If you see an animal for the first time and you don't know what kind of animal it is, you look at it without any memory, without any knowledge and you don't know how you will react. . . .

KRISHNAMURTI: Sir, you see, we have to go into this question of memory. I thought we had explained it enough! We cannot live without memory. Right? If you had no memory at all you would be in a state of amnesia and you wouldn't know what you were doing, your name or where you lived—nothing. Memory obviously has a place. We have killed each other in the name of God, in the name of peace, in the name of nationality for centuries; that is stored-up memory, and according to that memory we respond. And that response has produced disastrous results as well as very good results; scientifically it has produced an extraordinary world. But that memory also has produced appalling wars. We are concerned not with the good results of memory but with the destructive quality of a mind that

171

is conditioned. Right? Shall we proceed from there, not go back and back?

We are asking if it is possible for an action to take place in which there is no contradiction and no conflict. That is the question. An action which will not breed conflict within oneself, because we said conflict in any form is violence—conflict when I discipline myself according to a pattern, or suppress my feeling because of an ideal. Such discipline, such conformity is effort, is a contradiction which must breed violence. I think that is clear, isn't it? So we are asking, is there an action which is not the result of contradiction? Now, let's proceed to find out, not intellectually, not verbally, but actually, inwardly, find out for ourselves; which means we have to enquire into this whole field of consciousness. What is consciousness? What is thought? What is the observer who says, "I am thinking" and "this should be" and "that should not be"? Right? So let's proceed.

Is all consciousness the result of contradiction? You understand my question? Do I know a state of mind in which there is no contradiction at all? Am I aware of a state of being in which every form of conflict has ended? Or, do I only know conflict? You understand my question? Find out Sirs, we are taking the journey together, you're not just listening to my words. We are exploring together, exploring our state of mind.

Questioner: Does conflict arise because we give a meaning to things built through thought?

KRISHNAMURTI: Look, my question is this: I am conscious, I am conscious of this tent and the people in it, I am conscious that I am speaking, and I am aware of the limitation of my feelings and thoughts and I take cognizance of my limitation. And that limitation is my consciousness, in't it? No?

Questioner: What do you mean by "limitation," Sir?
172

KRISHNAMURTI: I am limited by my thought, I am limited by my feeling—my feelings are very small, my feelings are self-centered, my love is full of hate, jealousy and envy. And this is the consciousness in which I live.

Questioner: Without all this there is no conflict.

KRISHNAMURTI: Wait, wait, we're going to find out. Am I conscious only through my limitation? Am I conscious only of the content of this limitation? That is, I am aware of the content of myself—my thoughts, my feelings, my anxieties, my guilts, my hopes, despairs, loneliness—and because I am aware of the content, I am therefore aware of the limitation of my consciousness.

Questioner: But I'm aware of other things too, Sir, I see you there!

KRISHNAMURTI: Hold on to that for the moment.

Questioner: Do you mean, Sir, that the limitations you see are just what you want to see.

KRISHNAMURTI: No, no, no. It's not just what I want to see.

Questioner: You're creating a boundary with whatever it is you see—it's a boundary.

KRISHNAMURTI: Sir, may I ask you something? What to you is consciousness?

Questioner: Being awake.

KRISHNAMURTI: When do you know you're awake?

Questioner: I suppose when I have an experience.

KRISHNAMURTI: Be very simple. Go very simply into this. When do I know I am awake?

173

Questioner: I don't know I'm asleep. I remember that I was asleep, afterwards.

KRISHNAMURTI: Look, please Sir, let's think about this very simply. I go to sleep and I wake up to my daily routine, to my daily troubles, to my daily worries, to my daily apprehensions, fears, joys—I'm awake to those things. That's one part of it. I am also awake to all my motives—if I'm at all aware. Now, what makes me awake, keep awake? Are we pursuing this wrongly, in a wrong direction?

Questioner: The conflict and awareness of my limitations of thought keep me awake.

KRISHNAMURTI: Sir, look, if you have no conflict at all of any kind would you say, I'm awake?

Questioner: I think so. Are you saying that if there is no conflict or something like conflict. . . .

KRISHNAMURTI: No, no I did not say that, Sir. I asked: if you are not in conflict at all, at any level, what would that state be? Would you then say, I am awake? Or, do you only know you are awake through conflict?

Questioner: (in French) I am conscious when I am open to impressions (quand je me sens disponible).

KRISHNAMURTI: Sir, when are you conscious? Do stick to this for two minutes. When are you hurt? When you have joy, when you respond? Otherwise you're dead or asleep. So you only know that you are conscious, awake, when there is a challenge and a response. That's all! Wait, Sir, that's all we're saying. So, I am conscious only when there is a challenge to which I respond and that response breeds conflict. If the response is complete to the challenge there is no conflict. Then I don't even know that I'm responding, then I don't even know of the challenge, because I'm

174

so completely awake. Of course that sounds Utopian non-sense! I am pointing out only one thing, which is: I am awake only when there is challenge and response and that response is not complete to the challenge, is not adequate to that challenge. Right? Which means, when there is a challenge and I don't act completely or respond completely to that challenge, there is conflict. So I only know conflict, which makes me say "I am conscious." Now, wait a minute. When I say "I love you" is there conflict?

Questioner: What does love mean?

KRISHNAMURTI: Please Sir, don't analyze, we'll analyze it presently, just listen. When I say "I love you" is there conflict?

Questioner: Well, if there is conflict, then you're saying it when you're asleep.

KRISHNAMURTI: Quite right.

Questioner: Sir, in this business of being asleep all the time and dead all the time, there must be lapses when one's consciousness may not be like you describe. Could you point out a lapse so we could get the feel of it?

KRISHNAMURTI: Look, Sir, what are we trying to find out, what are we trying to do with each other? We are trying to find out whether violence, which is conflict, can come to an end. Right? Not superficially, but deeply. And in enquiring into that we are looking into the whole process of memory —into the state of mind which is perpetually in conflict. And because we are in conflict, we are in misery, we are conscious. Right? When you are completely happy—you follow Sir?—are you conscious that you're happy?

Questioner: There is a different kind of consciousness when you are happy.

175

KRISHNAMURTI: Don't introduce other factors, Sir, take just one fact.

Questioner: *But there are other factors.*

KRISHNAMURTI: I know, there are lots of other factors, I know that.

Questioner: *Then your question does not have any meaning.*

KRISHNAMURTI: It has no meaning if we bring in all the other factors, but I'm just asking a very simple question. When you're tremendously joyous are you conscious that you're joyous?

Questioner :(1) *No.*

Questioner (2): *Yes.*

Questioner (3): *You stop to look at it.*

KRISHNAMURTI: When you're very angry, at that second, are you conscious, or only afterwards? When, for whatever motive, there's an extraordinary state of happiness, you're not at that second, conscious. Later on it begins, you say, what an extraordinary moment that was, I wish I could have it repeated, and so on and so on. So both conflict and that state in which there is no conflict, is within this field of consciousness. Right? No?

Questioner: *(Somewhat inaudible). . . . a small child or an animal. . . .*

KRISHNAMURTI: Sir, we're not discussing the child or the animal, we are discussing ourselves—you and I—not the child nor the animal. Here I am. Look, Sir. Here I am, there you are—our problem is we have lived in violence for so many centuries. As human beings we are asking our selves: is it possible to be free of this violence? And in asking that question we are exploring; we're not going back to the child or to the animal. The animal is also violent and we have inherited perhaps that violence, or that violence has been created as the result of society, a culture. But we are violent and we're asking if that violence can come to an end—in you and in me.

Questioner: Is not consciousness the feeling of being separated from other human beings?

KRISHNAMURTI: Yes, Sir, that's part of it; when there is a separation between the observer and the observed.

Questioner: Sir, did you say that not being conscious at the moment of anger or passion, and the immediate memory of it, both those things are within the field of consciousness?

KRISHNAMURTI: Are they?

Questioner: They have to be, otherwise you could not remember.

KRISHNAMURTI: Of course. What are we asking, Sir? We are trying to find out the nature of conflict, conflict being violence. Now, this conflict in which we have lived has created a consciousness in which there is the observer and the observed. Right? There is the me and the not-me, which means there is a separation between the observer and the observed. Right? Now, will not this violence, this conflict endure as long as there is this separation?

Questioner: Separation and the conflict within ourselves will cease when we give up everything on earth.

KRISHNAMURTI: Sir, Sir, we're not giving up. That's just a theory; "when we give up everything on earth." We can't give up everything on this earth. We have to have food, we have to have clothes, shelter. Sir, let's make it very simple,

177

shall we? I want to be free of violence. How am I to do it? What am I to do? I have tried suppression, I have tried conformity, I have tried identifying myself with something greater which I call peace, love, God, and that doesn't solve it either—right? I have tried everything! Because I really want to be free of violence, because to me violence is a disease and a healthy mind must be free of every form of disease. So I say, what am I to do? Such obvious things as to give up my nationality, religious beliefs, dogmas—that's gone, finished—it has no meaning any more—but I'm still violent, I'm still aggressive, ambitious. Now I say: what am I to do?

Questioner: Conflict is the result of education. If you eliminate all those conflicts from education you're no longer alive.

KRISHNAMURTI: Yes, Sir, I understand, but answer me: will you tell me how to be free of violence? That's all I ask. I have tried education, I have tried religion, I have tried to control myself, I have tried to be kind and generous, yet there are moments when I am tremendously violent. My problem, my question is: what am I to do to be free of this violence?

Questioner: But this question is a subtle form of violence.

KRISHNAMURTI: No, no, it is not! Put it round the other way, Sir; I want to live completely at peace with myself and with the world—which doesn't mean I go to sleep, or go to a mountain, into a cave or some absurd thing, but I want to live peacefully. What am I to do?

Questioner: You can't do it.

KRISHNAMURTI: "You cannot"—then my problem is solved! I can't live at peace. But I *want* to live at peace! Look, please I beg of you, just listen. I want to live at peace—right?—it isn't just an idea, it isn't just a formula. I don't want to have a breath of hate, jealousy, anxiety, fear in me. I want to live completely at peace! Which doesn't mean I want to die. I want to live in this world, I want to function, I want to look at the trees, flowers, women, boys, girls—I want to look at them and at the same time live completely at peace with myself and with the world. What am I to do? But you don't ask that question; you're asking all kinds of questions. When you ask that question what do you reply? Either you say like that gentleman, "you can't," therefore you have blocked yourself, you have stopped yourself from further enquiry; or you say you can be at peace only when you go to Heaven, that is, when you die.

Questioner: You are left only to stand still. . . .

KRISHNAMURTI: No, I don't want to stand still, I want to live, I am living, I want to love without hate, without jealousy.

Questioner: Your problem is to communicate your wish to the world, only then will you have the possibility of having peace.

KRISHNAMURTI: Ah, no. I don't want to communicate with the world; the world is stupid, the world is brutal. How can I communicate with the world? Sir, you are just talking nonsense.

Questioner: You must be vulnerable.

KRISHNAMURTI: You're just quoting what I said yesterday. That's not my argument. I don't want to have conflict within myself at any cost, I don't want to quarrel with anybody; I want to have great affection, kindliness, love—I don't want anything else.

Questioner: It's not true for me.

KRISHNAMURTI: It may not be true for you; then if it is not true for you, why isn't it true for you?

179

Questioner: Well, I wish it were.

KRISHNAMURTI: Look, we started this discussion by asking ourselves if it is possible to be free of violence. To be free of violence means to live at peace—right?—and if I say I don't want to live at peace, I want to carry on with violence, there is something totally wrong with such a mind.

Questioner: I don't say I don't want peace; I say, I see my wish for violence.

KRISHNAMURTI: What are you to do, Sir? You want peace, I want peace; I don't want to have a single breath of conflict in me at any time—sleeping or waking—what am I to do?

Questioner: Respond to the challenge of life.

KRISHNAMURTI: Please, would you ask that question yourselves? My question to you, which I have put to you: do you really want to live at peace with yourself, which means no conflict?

Questioner: I will repeat again, you cannot live without violence, it's only an idea that you want to live without violence.

KRISHNAMURTI: No, no, it is not an idea.

Questioner: But it's an idea that you want to live without violence.

KRISHNAMURTI: Please Sir, I have lived in conflict all my life (I haven't personally, but it doesn't matter) I have lived in conflict with my wife, with my children, with my society, with my boss, with everything, and I say to myself: is there a way of living in which there is no conflict? It is not an idea!

180

Questioner: Sorry, but this question is not the most important thing; the most important thing is to see violence. That takes time.

KRISHNAMURTI: No, no, we have been through that Sir. We have discussed the nature of violence, we have been into that and I'm putting the same question differently. I want to live in this world, not as an idea but actually, every minute of my life, I want to live in a different way, in which there is no conflict, which means no violence. Will you put this question to yourself, Sir? Don't answer me. Put this question to yourself.

Questioner: But we are discussing.

KRISHNAMURTI: Of course, Sir, we are discussing, but first put this question—see what happens to you—then find out what your response is.

Questioner: (inaudible)

KRISHNAMURTI: That's a lovely idea—"when, when I am" —I won't discuss it!

Questioner: We don't know enough. . . .

KRISHNAMURTI: Have you ever put this question to yourself? You know what conflict is, not as an idea, but what actually takes place when you quarrel with your wife or husband, when you are frightened of the boss, when you are frightened of every kind of thing—there is conflict. And have you asked yourselves if it is possible to live without conflict, not as an ideal, but actually?

Questioner: Can you divide your soul from your body?

KRISHNAMURTI: This is a question which is not relevant to the point. Look, I'm asking you, do please have the goodness to listen. Humanity has lived in conflict for centuries. Is that the way to live? If it is, then all right, let's go on. If it is not, then is there a way of living in which there is no conflict at all? Put that question to yourself, not as an idea but as a thing that you want to find out.

Questioner: We don't know....

KRISHNAMURTI: Madame, I'm not saying you should know. Put that question, see what you find out.

Questioner: Our mind is conditioned so how can we know?

Questioner (2): Can we have ten minutes of silence?

KRISHNAMURTI: No, please, first put the question to yourself.

Questioner: If I am not mature enough it is impossible to put this question.

KRISHNAMURTI: Then, why aren't you mature? Who's going to make you mature?

Questioner: I am not mature....

KRISHNAMURTI: But Sir, that is not my question. Put that question, see what happens. Find out that you are immature. We are avoiding the question, that's all.

Questioner: Shouldn't it be a question for everyone, and everybody should keep the answer to himself?

KRISHNAMURTI: Keep it to yourself, I'm not asking you to tell me. Put it, and find out what your answer is. Find out how far you will go, how far you will go to live peacefully.
182

Questioner: At the same moment as you realize, deep in yourself, that this whole world leads nowhere, in fact this realization brings in yourself a "stop". . . .

KRISHNAMURTI: It's really quite an extraordinary phenomenon this, isn't it? You're all so ready to answer, which means that you have not really put this question to yourself. Perhaps you dare not put the question.

Questioner: (In Italian) But I have to start with something I have heard, something someone said about a different state. But all I see is the conflict, and I don't know if there is a way out.

KRISHNAMURTI: Yes, Sir, but that's not my point. My point is: you have lived in conflict and don't you ask yourself, is that the only thing I have to live for—conflict, conflict? It is not a different state that you want to achieve; but here I am in conflict and is there a way out of it?

Questioner: Sir, I think there's only conflict between persons, you and another person or a group of people and when you study them, when you "are" the other persons, see what they are trying to do, what you're trying to do, see the whole thing dispassionately, this will produce an easier situation; it may not remove conflict but it is a step towards it.

KRISHNAMURTI: Sir, put the question the other way. Don't you want to stop wars, which means, don't you want to live peacefully every day, to put an end to war?

Questioner: But just as all wars are fought to end wars, isn't the desire to end conflict the prime generator of conflict?

KRISHNAMURTI: That is one of the old sayings, Sir—this war is not like the last war, it is to end all wars—you understand?

183

Questioner: Do you have a method for ending war?

KRISHNAMURTI: Sir, what a question to ask; you have heard me often, haven't you, Sir?

Questioner: You asked "do you want to end war"? So I asked, "do you have a method"?

KRISHNAMURTI: But you have heard me often, haven't you, Sir?

Questioner: Yes, Sir.

KRISHNAMURTI: Therefore you will find the answer if you have heard me.

Questioner: Sir, whichever way one's mind moves, when you ask yourself that question, then you see that the projection the mind makes is not going to give the answer. . . .

KRISHNAMURTI: Look, how far are you willing to go to have peace in your life?

Questioner: All the way.

KRISHNAMURTI: What does that mean? That means to end conflict, doesn't it? Now, how do you end conflict? Keep it very simple, Sir. How do you end conflict in yourself and live ordinarily? Is it possible?

Questioner: All I can say is that it has not been possible.

KRISHNAMURTI: Why? Go into it, Sir, don't answer me, necessarily. I don't want to quarrel with you—so I stop quarreling.

Questioner: (inaudible)
184

KRISHNAMURTI: Wait, wait. I quarrel with you because you want my wife, or I quarrel with you because you want my position; I quarrel with you because I'm jealous of you, I quarrel with you because you're much more intelligent than I am, and so on. Am I willing to stop quarreling with you altogether? Willing to do it? When you run away with my wife I won't quarrel with you.

Questioner: But quarreling is inside the mind as well as outside.

KRISHNAMURTI: I'm talking of "inside," not outside.

Questioner: I don't control my thought-stream. . . .

KRISHNAMURTI: No Sir, it doesn't bang into you. So I have to understand myself—right? I don't want to quarrel with you under any circumstance. I want to live peacefully with you; if you want my shirt I'll give it to you. Fortunately I have no property and if you want that property you can have it; but I won't quarrel with you. If you want to come and sit on the platform and I sit there, you're welcome, I won't quarrel with you. I'm not ambitious, I'm not greedy, I don't want any of those things, because I don't want to quarrel with you. To me, what is important is not to quarrel, therefore the other things subside. To quarrel like so many monkeys, like animals, is uncivilized, immoral in the deep sense. I feel that very strongly, therefore I'll do it. So, Sir, it all boils down to one thing: how deeply, how fundamentally do we want to live without violence? How deeply do we want to live at peace with each other? We may say we want it—but actually! And that's why it's very important to go within oneself, to find out the nature and the structure of one's being. Therefore, one has to know oneself. Perhaps we can discuss this question of knowing oneself tomorrow.

4th August 1967

185

4

WE SAID YESTERDAY that we would go on talking about the question of knowing oneself. We have been discussing the problem of violence, and to understand it fully one has to comprehend the whole structure of the self, the me: what I actually am. Therefore it seems to me important to go into the question of knowing oneself. Because, if I do not understand myself completely, I have no basis for rational thinking; I have no foundation for action, I have no roots in what is virtue. Unless I understand myself, I am always in contradiction, in confusion and hence in conflict and misery. And being in conflict, in sorrow, inevitably that must express itself in some form of violence. So it seems to me very important to understand oneself, not according to any specialist, or to any religious concept of what is *the* "me," or the self, but actually to become aware of it as it operates, as it functions. But if I try to understand myself according to some philosopher or psychologist, then I am trying to understand *them*: what they think about me, what they think is my structure, my nature.

Most of us are second-hand human beings and there is nothing original in us (not that we are seeking any originality). But merely to operate in a second-hand way without any original feeling or any original understanding must inevitably lead to conflicts, miseries and endless anxieties. So I hope you and I (the speaker as well as yourself) see the importance of knowing ourselves. If we both agree that it is vital to understand ourselves completely, then we have a quite different relationship, then we can walk together, then we can both delve into the most secret corners of our minds. But if you are not interested then I am afraid all communication between the speaker and yourself comes to an end.

There are several questions that have been sent such as: "I would like to live at peace, but to live at peace means I must give up food, clothes and shelter, which means I must die and if I die the violent people will create a society." This kind of question is really quite inadmissible, because we have talked enough about the necessity of food, clothes and shelter and whether it is possible to live in this world of brutality at peace with ourselves; so I won't go into such questions.

So, if we could this morning devote our whole energy to understand ourselves and go to the very end of it (not just give up if we don't like it) then perhaps we shall discover for ourselves a state of mind that is not in conflict at all and therefore can live in this world at peace, both outwardly and inwardly. So, shall we converse together about this question of understanding ourselves?

Where do we begin to understand ourselves? Here I am, and how am I to study myself, observe myself, see what is actually taking place in myself? I can only observe myself in relationship, because all life is relationship. If I reject all relationship and isolate myself, become a hermit, even then I have relationship; I live in relationship, so I can only understand myself in observing my relationship to ideas, to people, to things. Right? What do you say?

Questioner: (in French) For the mind to perceive, energy is needed. Does this energy come from silence?

KRISHNAMURTI: But Sir, if you don't mind, that's not what we are discussing this morning. What we are trying to find out is, how to understand oneself. Here I am, a bundle of contradictions, miseries, conflicts, anxieties, hopes, wishing to have a silent mind; I am a whole bundle of energy in contradiction. I want to understand myself because I see that without understanding myself there is no basis for any action; I can act, but it will always result in greater misery, greater confusion. So I must understand myself. Now where shall I begin? And I see I cannot exist by myself, I exist always in relationship, whether conscious or unconscious. That relationship is with people, with various ideologies, or with things, money, houses, furniture, food. In studying my relationship with these things, with outward things as well as inward things, I begin to understand myself. Is this clear?

Questioner: When I observe myself I see myself in very different states. Is the self a reality, or not?

KRISHNAMURTI: We're going to find out. Look, will you do something this morning? Forget all that you know about yourself; forget all that you have thought about yourself. We're starting to find out; we are going to start as though we knew nothing. Then it is worthwhile. But if you start with all the old furniture that you have collected for the last thirty years you can't travel very far. So let us begin as though we were on a new journey.

It rained last night heavily and the skies are beginning to clear; it's a new day, a fresh dawn, and you must meet that fresh day as though it were the only day. But if you meet it with all the remembrance of yesterday, you will never meet the freshness of today. So what we are doing now is to start to understand ourselves for the first time. And I see I can only understand myself in relation to people, things and ideas. I cannot understand myself sitting in a corner, meditating about myself, or withdrawing, isolating myself in some monastery. I can only understand myself in relationship; because every other form is merely an abstraction and has no validity at all. If we could start with that, each one of us, then we'll go far, but if we start with abstractions—what should be, how to keep the mind silent, all the things that you have heard this unfortunate speaker say—then you'll be lost. Whereas if this morning we could go step by step into this, you will discover many things for yourself.

Questioner: When I'm aware of what's happening in me. . . .

KRISHNAMURTI: No, Sir, you've gone far ahead of me. I said you can only understand yourself in relationship. Right?

Questioner: Yes, but what puzzles me is, what you mean by relationship.

KRISHNAMURTI: We're going to go into it. You see, it's a fresh morning, Sir. First, let's be clear that I can understand myself only by studying my relationship and my reactions in those relationships. I am related to things: property and material things. What is my reaction towards those things, to money, to clothes, to food, to houses? By studying my reactions I am beginning to understand myself in relation to those things. Right? Are we doing that? You have a relationship to your house, to your property, to property as the family—and that's a very complex question, how you react to your property, to things. Don't brush it aside; this is very important to understand. Suppose I have plenty of money, what is my relationship to that thing called money? By understanding my reaction I understand myself. My reaction is myself. Right? So I'm beginning to see very clearly what my reaction is with regard to money; whether I hate rich people because I'm poor, or I want to be as rich as the rich man.

So I begin to study myself through my reaction to things. I need food, clothes and shelter, that's absolutely necessary. But what is my reaction to them? Do they give me an inner satisfaction—you understand?—an inner security? If so, I attach tremendous importance to property, therefore I'm willing to defend my property. And defending my property I'm violent, and therefore I create a society in which, through money, I gain tremendous satisfaction. I've discovered a tremendous lot about myself. Are you doing this with me? I discover that I'm using property, things—which I need, which are necessary—as a means of inward security, satisfaction, and therefore property becomes extraordinarily important. Right? Ah, wait—don't say no! Please, it is not a question of saying yes or no; we are studying ourselves by our reaction to things. Do I use property as a status symbol? I'm beginning to understand myself in relation to things—what is my relationship to things—relationship—you understand? To have a relationship means to be related to, to be in contact with—doesn't it? May I go on? Am I in contact with property, with things, or, am I in contact with the satisfaction which things give me, therefore I use things to gain satisfaction, and so things become of secondary importance, because my primary desire is to find satisfaction, to have security? Right? And I discover something very odd about myself— that I want property, things, and also I see the danger of it, and I want to avoid it; I want to put it aside and yet I want to hold it. Right? So contradiction in me has already begun. I like to have a lovely house, nice garden, lots of servants, and that gives me a tremendous sense of security, position, prestige, an inward gratification. I use things for my own gratification, therefore I protect those things which give me the satisfaction and hence I am in a state of defense all the time.

Questioner: (in French) I don't see the importance of knowing myself, but hearing you explain that it is important, I then discover that it is important—is this not an escape?

KRISHNAMURTI: You discover the importance of knowing yourself because someone has asserted that it is important. You don't see the importance for yourself. Why don't you see it? It's like a man living in blindness and saying, it's not important to have eyes. Are you being stimulated by the speaker, who lays emphasis on understanding oneself, to be interested in that? Then it has no value at all.

All right Sir, let's proceed: I discover myself in relationship to things because to us things are extraordinarily important. Don't let's fool ourselves. Money, houses, material things that you touch, feel, taste, are extraordinarily important. And why have they become important? Please follow this. Why have they become important to me or to you? I need food, I need shelter, I need clothes, but why have they become of such colossal importance in life? What do you say Sirs?

Questioner: *They become important to us because we are empty inside.*

KRISHNAMURTI: In ourselves we are nothing, so we fill that emptiness with furniture—no, no, don't laugh—with books, with money, with cars. Right? So they become important, because they fill my state of mind which is completely dull, empty. Are we doing that?

Questioner: *Sir, I don't think that's a conscious reason for it.*

KRISHNAMURTI: I don't know. Sir, you are discovering yourself, you're not telling me.

Questioner: *Well, to me, my conscious reason is that I see very poor people and all sorts of misery—they can't pay the doctor and so on—and I don't want to be like that. And what keeps me from being like that? It's the material things, so therefore the objects acquire a great importance.*

191

KRISHNAMURTI: Yes Sir, we said that: it is of very great importance.

Questioner: *That's the reason why we give them importance.*

KRISHNAMURTI: That's one of the reasons. That's not the major reason. One of the reasons is that I don't want to be like the poor man, therefore I defend what I have. Right? Therefore I'm in a state of violence. I have discovered that; you're not telling me, I'm not telling you. I have discovered by comparison that it is better to be well off. You're more respected, you become a respectable bourgeois and all the rest of it. We are still examining (you understand, Sir?) I'm studying myself. When I use things to cover my own insufficiency, to cover my own emptiness, shallowness, my own shoddiness of being, with furniture, with houses, with name, with all that, what happens? Pursue that. What happens in this process?

Questioner: *But this problem about which you have spoken now, the attraction to objects in order to fill our emptiness, I think this is psychological, and has its origin in more concrete things. If we take an animal for instance. . . .*

KRISHNAMURTI: Ah, I don't want to take an animal.

Questioner: *I know from my own experience that without food I'm violent.*

KRISHNAMURTI: But Sir, we have said that. I need food, I need shelter, I need clothes. There is no question about that. Every animal needs them.

Questioner: *Hence my attachment—it is due to fear.*

KRISHNAMURTI: Yes Sir, but why are we attached? I must have those things. Why do I give them such extraordinary importance?

192

Questioner: But I feel that if I do not have them I will die.

KRISHNAMURTI: Of course, of course, so you give them such tremendous importance. Is that the reason you give importance to food, clothes and shelter? Find out, Sir, in yourself.

Questioner: (in French) Money is a symbol, but in fact it is part of the organization of material life on which the spiritual life is based. One must study it and understand the intricate part money plays in life and its meaning.

KRISHNAMURTI: That is not the question, but what is my relationship to it. I want to know my relationship to things: to money, to houses, to food, clothes and shelter. In that way I shall find out about myself. That's what we are discussing; not how money conditions us. Of course it conditions; the man who has no money is conditioned by not having it, and the man who has got money is also conditioned. We know that Sir.

Questioner: (in French) We need material things, but why is it that we are empty without them?

KRISHNAMURTI: Why should I be empty? No, Sir, look—we are studying ourselves. I am saying to myself: I want to understand myself and therefore I can understand myself only in relationship to things, to people and to ideas. Probably there is only one relationship, which is the relationship I have in regard to ideas, and that is the only thing that matters—ideas. You follow Sir? Not food, not people, but the image, the symbol I have about food, clothes, shelter and people. Right? There's nothing wrong in having food, clothes and shelter, but it is the idea I have about it. So I have a relationship, not with things or with people but only with symbols and ideas. Is that so? Do you find that out?

Questioner: I think, Sir, that we identify ourselves with things and they become part of us.

KRISHNAMURTI: Yes, Sir, we identify ourselves with things and therefore they become part of us.

Questioner: When I get a lot of money for myself I feel great pleasure for a moment and then the pleasure dies and I must go and get something else. It seems that there is only an image, because when I have the object, it doesn't continue to give pleasure, so there must again be the idea of getting more and this goes on and one is never satisfied.

KRISHNAMURTI: I am learning that really things don't matter at all, nor people, but what matters immensely is my ideas about things and people.

Questioner: Sir, the relation I have with the idea is the relation between me and myself, because the idea is a part of myself.

KRISHNAMURTI: No, no. That is a conclusion. You've already decided you're the projection of yourself, therefore you're identified with the projection and therefore you're continuing yourself. But that doesn't help me to understand myself. Sir, put it round the other way. What is most important to me and to you? Look at yourself, please. Not money, food, clothes and shelter, but what it will give you. Right? You have an image, a symbol, an idea about this—about property and about people. Are you related to people? Am I related to people, to my friend, to my wife, to my husband? Or am I related to the image which I have created for myself about people?

Questioner: It's a habit.

KRISHNAMURTI: All right, it's a habit. Why have I created this habit? Why am I not directly in relationship with things—with property—we'll call it that for the moment—and with people? Why should I have ideas? And if you say "that's a habit," then how did that habit come into being? Why am I a slave to this habit?

Questioner: *Because I'm not lively enough.*

KRISHNAMURTI: Don't say, I'm not lively enough. You and I are trying to understand ourselves, so please don't come to any conclusions, or say "I should be, I am not but I should be." All that has no meaning. In studying myself in relation to property, to people, I see what is tremendously important to me. Much more important than people or property are the ideas, the feelings, the images I have about them. Right?

Questioner: *(in Italian: inaudible)*

KRISHNAMURTI: No, Sir. Go into it a little more slowly. Why have things not their own value, people their own value, why do I put greater value on the images, thoughts, ideas I have about them? Why? You've understood, Sir? You're not important at all—what is important to me is my idea about you, my image about you. Why have I created this image? If you say, "it's a habit," all right it's a habit. But why am I caught in this habit, how did this habit come into being?

Questioner: *Because life has frightened me.*

KRISHNAMURTI: Therefore, I am living in abstractions. Right? Not in reality, but in abstractions. Therefore, my relationship to you is an abstraction. I am not actually related. I live in abstractions, in ideas, in images, and I say: why have I done this? Why have I created the image about you?

Questioner: *Could it be that the basic reason is that. . . .*

KRISHNAMURTI: Don't be abstract, find out!

Questioner: Well, I'm looking! The basic reason is that I am convinced that possessing the object will give me satisfaction.

KRISHNAMURTI: No, Sir. Go into it a little deeper, you will find out. Look at it quietly. Don't verbalize yet, but just look at it. Here I am, I have given tremendous significance to things, to people, but what is much more important to me is not things or people, but the ideas I have about them. And why have I made this more important than things and people?

Questioner: To protect myself.

KRISHNAMURTI: Do look, wait, Sir. Take two minutes and look at it. I am studying myself, not passing an exam. I say, "why have I done this?" Why have not only I, but all human beings done this? Whether they live in Asia or in Europe or in America, why have human beings done this?

Questioner: Sir, I think that the object itself, or the person, is for us too complicated to understand and therefore we create an image which is much simpler and easier to handle.

KRISHNAMURTI: I have an image about you because the image is very simple, but you are very complicated. You are a living thing—moving, active, throbbing—and I cannot understand you, therefore I create a symbol about you. All the churches are filled with symbols, because a symbol is a dead thing. I can clothe it, I can put garlands around it, I can do anything I like, but I can't do that with a living thing.

Questioner: Words in themselves are symbols.

KRISHNAMURTI: Of course.

Questioner: I have an image of myself when I look at you, and then. . . .

KRISHNAMURTI: Please Sir, we are studying ourselves. We are looking at ourselves and trying to understand ourselves, the reason being that without understanding ourselves we must always be in a state of confusion. Without understanding myself I must be violent; without understanding myself there is no virtue. So I must understand myself! And I say: in looking at myself, nothing matters at all except my ideas about things! Right?

Questioner: (in French) We must find a "milieu" that suits us and will let us flower.

KRISHNAMURTI: You're going away from the point. To every human being—I see it in myself and I see it in you—ideas are much more important than things or people. Nationalism is an idea! And for that I'm willing to kill, destroy myself and lose my property.

Questioner: Giving importance to things is really to the ideas attached to those things. But we do also give importance to actual things.

KRISHNAMURTI: The same thing Sir, isn't it?

Questioner: We don't tell ourselves that the idea is important, we tell ourselves the thing or the person is important, but the importance which we give to the thing or the person is idea.

KRISHNAMURTI: If course, that's what we are saying.

Questioner: Would you include among the things your own philosophizing?

KRISHNAMURTI: I am not philosophizing. If I were it would be included among things—to be thrown out of the window. Sir, you're going away all the time. Let us stick to this point. Here I am, I want to understand myself. In that understanding I've discovered something: that to me people are important and that involves ideas and I am attached to ideas. Now, I ask myself, why has this taken place.

Questioner: It's a kind of defense against something new—I neutralize things, cover them with my ideas. . . .

KRISHNAMURTI: That means, you're neutralizing, you're blocking, you're denying the living thing, but not your idea—doesn't it? You are a living thing—your wife, your husband, you—and to live with you without idea means living without the image; I have to be on my toes all the time. Right? I have to watch you. I can't have an image about you because it would prevent me from watching you. I have to watch your moods, your speech, the way you talk, I have to watch everything, and that becomes tremendously exacting, arduous. Therefore, it is much simpler to hold on to my image about you.

Questioner: (in French) There are times when things have more importance than ideas—such as in a moment of danger.

KRISHNAMURTI: All right Sir, let's proceed. Only with regard to dead things I have no ideas, but I have ideas which protect me in my relationship with you as a husband, wife, friend—whatever it is—because you are much too active. So what has happened? I have an image about you which I have built and I keep on adding to that image. Right? Watch yourself, Sir! What happens in that state? I have an image about you and I live with that image. You become an abstraction; you're not real. My image about you is real. What happens then? What is my relationship to you? Have I any relationship to you at all?

Questioner: There's a destructive quality in what you are saying.

KRISHNAMURTI: No, Madame, watch yourself please. I am living in relationship with you—at least I think I am living in relationship with you—but actually I'm living with the image which I have put together about you. So I am living in the past. And you're also living in the past. Because you have an image about me and I have an image about you, and these two images have a relationship. Right, Sirs? Then what takes place, what actually takes place?

Questioner: Conflict takes place.

KRISHNAMURTI: Conflict?

Questioner: Conflict, between the idea and the fact.

KRISHNAMURTI: The questioner says, "there is conflict between the fact—you—and the image, which is non-fact." And hence, there is conflict. Wait, wait, watch yourselves. Go into yourselves.

Questioner: Life is a flow and the image is static.

KRISHNAMURTI: All right, is that a discovery you have made?

Questioner: Yes.

KRISHNAMURTI: Then what next? If you have found that, what happens? Then you say, "I see that I'm always living in the past." And life, which is moving, living, is always in the present, therefore I look at you with dead eyes. Right?

Questioner: Not especially with dead eyes; because if I want to understand a statue I turn it around but I cannot understand the whole statue. I always have only an image.

KRISHNAMURTI: Yes, Sir, that's what we are saying.

Questioner: How can one discover with a mind which is held in the past?

KRISHNAMURTI: We are going to go into that step by step.

Questioner: Why do I need to create images about everything?

KRISHNAMURTI: That's what we are asking Sir. Is it that we are creating images because we are frightened of this thing that is living? Watch it, Sir! Is that so in you?

Questioner: If only I were satisfied with the direct impact, but I seem to want something else.

KRISHNAMURTI: Yes, go ahead, add.

Questioner: If I were to try and find satisfaction by touching the deeper things as they are, I would find that this whole world is very annoying.

KRISHNAMURTI: Of course, that's part of it. . . . I'm bored, I'm frightened—it's all in that field. Now, why do I do this? Go a little deeper. I realize I'm doing this. Why am I doing this?

Questioner (1): It is seeking pleasure.

Questioner (2): Is it a process of building up a protective camouflage to hide what actually happens?

KRISHNAMURTI: Yes, Sir, quite right. But why am I doing it?

Questioner: Because I can't live in the present.

KRISHNAMURTI: Yes, Sir. Are you answering me? Or are you understanding it yourself?

Questioner: Isn't the question: why do we always keep the memories alive?

KRISHNAMURTI: Yes, Sir. Why?

Questioner: When I think of something it will lead either to the past or to the future. . . .

KRISHNAMURTI: Quite right.

Questioner: The image gives a relationship to the past or to the future, not to the present.

KRISHNAMURTI: Quite right, Sir. I agree, then what? I saw a sunset yesterday, it was a great pleasure, a great joy, and it has left a mark and this evening I look at the light on the hill with the eyes of yesterday, with the memories of yesterday. I'm doing this all the time. Why am I doing it? Go deeper Sir, go into it. Don't just verbalize it immediately.

Questioner: Because without memories one would be nothing.

KRISHNAMURTI: Is that what you have learnt?

Questioner: Sir, I don't think I know reality. I see things always through images, so I don't really know what reality is.

KRISHNAMURTI: Yes. Why? Please, we have explained enough. Just stop for a few minutes and find out why you are doing this. One says it is pleasure, the other says it is "emptiness." One says it is fear, the others says "it is habit." and so on. But go below the words, below the immediate discovery and understanding, go below that.

201

Questioner: If you watch a child. . . .

KRISHNAMURTI: I don't want to watch a child. Here I am.

Questioner: One minute it is satisfied with one thing, and then with another. . . .

KRISHNAMURTI: I know that, Sir.

Questioner: I do the same in a more complicated way.

KRISHNAMURTI: Why am I doing this, why am I building images? Why can't I live with the living thing all the time—the living thing is moving, acting, it may be wrong, it may be right, but why can't I live with *that?*

Questioner: Who is building the images?

KRISHNAMURTI: I'm coming to that, Sir. First see, go slowly, you'll come upon it yourself.

Questioner: Is there anybody there? Is there anybody building?

KRISHNAMURTI: You're going to find out.

Questioner: Can the living thing exist for me at all without the image, Sir?

KRISHNAMURTI: Please listen to that question. Can the living thing—you—exist at all if I have no ideas about you? How quickly you answer, Sir. Does your wife live without your idea about her? Of course she does.

Questioner: But not for me. Do I have any other cognizance of her existence?

KRISHNAMURTI: You have an image about the speaker, haven't you? You have, unfortunately. Now, why do you
202

have that image? The image built on reputation, propaganda, all that. Why have you got that image? Why can't you be directly in relationship with the speaker? Why do you have to have an image about him? Madame, do listen. How quick we are! Why can't you have a little patience to look?

Questioner: Because if I have the image and you are changing it is so difficult. . . .

KRISHNAMURTI: We said that. It is a protective reaction against a living thing. But why are we doing it?

Questioner: The image is a thought.

KRISHNAMURTI: Why is thought building the image? You are studying yourself; you're not waiting for an answer from me.

Questioner: All my thought can do is just that; that's all it ever does.

Questioner: As long as we look and experience from a fragment, we are keeping the image alive. But if we could see the totality then we would be free of it.

KRISHNAMURTI: No, Sir, that's not my question—not being free of anything. I am asking myself, why am I doing this all the time.

Questioner: I do not want to use initiative.

KRISHNAMURTI: You see, you're not answering my question, you haven't discovered for yourself, you're not studying yourself.

Questioner: But to face reality directly would be intolerable.

KRISHNAMURTI: We have said that, Sir, wait a minute. I want to find out why I am doing this. Why, when I look at a sunset today, the past sunset comes into my mind, and when I look at you—husband, wife, children, brother, whoever it is—I look at you through the image which I have about you—about clothes, about food, about everything. I live in abstraction and I say to myself, I know this, but why am I doing it? Now how do I find out?

Questioner: *By watching ourselves.*

KRISHNAMURTI: How do you watch yourselves?

Questioner: *Your reactions, your thoughts. . . .*

KRISHNAMURTI: We've been through that, Sir. Now I'm watching myself to find out why I create this image?

Questioner: *Because we're holding on to it.*

KRISHNAMURTI: No Sir. Watch it.

Questioner: *I seem to keep doing it, because I'm not aware I'm making images.*

KRISHNAMURTI: First, I'm not aware that I'm building the image, but when I do become aware, then I ask myself— "why am I doing this?" Please Sir, would you listen for two minutes quietly? I've asked this question and it's very important for me to find out. You can't answer it for me. I have to find out for myself. Now, how am I going to find out?

Questioner: *The image itself is showing me.*

KRISHNAMURTI: Madame, I said, give me a chance. Let me speak for two minutes. It's very important for me to find out. I don't want you to tell me at all, because if you tell me I say, "that might be it," and I might try to imitate or
204

follow that and say, "well it must be that." I don't want any of your suggestions. I want to find out for myself, as you *must*—for yourself. How do you do that? First, I must stop listening to your chattering as well as to my chattering. Right? I must stop listening to you—all your suggestions— and also I must stop listening to all my machinations, my fabrications. Do you agree? That means—what?

Questioner: Looking, Sir. Just looking.

KRISHNAMURTI: How do I look? Don't quote me. How do I look? I can only look when I am fairly quiet. Having asked myself and said, "I must find out why I create this image," am I then quiet or am I restlessly searching for an answer?

Questioner: If you're looking, Sir, then thought never interferes.

KRISHNAMURTI: Sir, please forgive me. I know I must be aware. I know I must observe. But to observe, to be aware I must be fairly quiet, mustn't I? That's all. I've asked the question, "why do I build up these images?" After having asked that question I must be quiet, mustn't I? Are we— are you—quiet? Or are you waiting for somebody to tell you? If you're quiet, and you are aware in that quietness, what is your response?

Questioner: Isn't there simply awareness?

KRISHNAMURTI: But I haven't understood why I have built this image.

Questioner: It seems that you are the only person who is going to be able to answer your question.

KRISHNAMURTI: Not at all! I don't want to take that responsibility. I'll answer it for myself.

Questioner: Sir, may it not be that thought keeps interven-ing; this thought is our memory, our conditioning, and if we are aware of that—aware of ourselves—then we (the "I") don't exist any more?

KRISHNAMURTI: Sir. Here is a problem, say a mathematical problem. I have searched every means to find out why I do it, in every avenue, and I can't find an answer, what do I do?

Questioner: I leave it.

KRISHNAMURTI: You leave it, or, as I don't want to leave it, I can't just drop it, I want to find out *now*.

Questioner: You must pause.

KRISHNAMURTI: Yes, you must pause, you must wait. Are you doing it?

Questioner: There's nothing for it but to realize that one doesn't know anything about it.

KRISHNAMURTI: Now we're off. Do you pause, do you keep quiet, wait, look?

Questioner: How can I be quiet when asking this ques-tion? It is still troubling me.

KRISHNAMURTI: Listen. You have asked a question. And how do you find the answer? You can't keep on asking, asking. You say, "yes, I have asked it, now I want to see where the answer is." Right? So you leave the question. You say, "now, to find an answer, to look, I must have a pause, there must be a lag, there must be quietness to look."

Questioner: But where is the asking in this lag? I forget the asking?

KRISHNAMURTI: Have I? I've finished with it. I've asked and I say, "I want to find out why I am building this image." I've asked it. I can't keep on asking. How am I going to find out? Who is going to tell me? You? If you tell me, will it be real to me? It's only real if I can find out for myself, and to find out for myself there must be no bias, no prejudice, no tension, no saying, "the answer must be this or that"; therefore I must be quiet, mustn't I? Which means thought must not interfere! Thought which has created the image. Right? And the image which thought has created is old because thought is always old. Therefore I see that and say, "the moment thought interferes I shan't find the real answer."

Questioner: *Instead of thought we should be filled with love.*

KRISHNAMURTI: I'm afraid I cannot fill myself with love; I don't know what it means.

Questioner: *All right Sir, I think we followed you up to this point.*

KRISHNAMURTI: Good! Now let's proceed. I have found that thought creates this image and thought is interfering and so prevents the discovery of *what is*, why I create these images. Right? Why does thought interfere at all? So my problem is not why the mind creates these images, but why does thought, which is the creator of the image, constantly interfere?

Questioner: *Then thought forms the ego. . . .*

KRISHNAMURTI: Thought forms the image; don't bring in a new word, otherwise it will get complicated. We are saying simply: thought has created the image, the image which I have built in my relationship with you, and that thought says to itself, now I must find out why I'm doing it. Thought is active. Right Sir? So thought thinks it will find out—go slowly, wait—so thought says, I have built this, I don't know why I have built it, but now I must find out. Thought thinks it will find out. What it will find out is an image which it has projected from past experience, therefore it is not a discovery, it is merely an activity of thought.

Questioner: Thought cannot have an answer.

KRISHNAMURTI: Yes, Sir, that's what we said. Can you keep thought quiet? Can thought say to itself, look I have done the mischief now I will be quiet?

Questioner: Sir, if we really go into it deeply then we will see that thought cannot find an answer.

KRISHNAMURTI: But why don't you see it? I have created an image about you through thinking about you, either pleasurably or because you have given me pain. Thought has created the image about you, through pleasure or through pain. Then I say to myself, why am I doing this? I ask that question and that question is asked by thought and thought is going to answer the question. So thought, if it answers the question, will be in the same category as the image. Right?

Questioner: But thought is not operating alone, it is operating with our feelings, all our psyche. We may say very easily that our thoughts are dictated by our feelings—that happens very often.

KRISHNAMURTI: Yes, Sir, we have said all that.

Questioner: Sir, can we go a little bit more slowly now?

KRISHNAMURTI: I am doing it, Sir.

Questioner: When thought discovers that it is the same thing as the image—can we look at that still more carefully?

KRISHNAMURTI: I'll do it Sir. Say, I am married to you and I have built an image about you—sexual pleasure, or the insulting things you have said to me, the nagging, the flattery, the hurts—all that has gone to build up an image about you. Who has done this? Thought, thinking about the sexual pleasure, thought thinking about the insult, thought thinking about the flattery you say, "How nice you look today, I like your looks! I adore you when you say that!"—so I have collected all that and I have created an image about you. The *I* is the thought. Right Sir? Wait. So thought has done this and thought is an abstraction, whereas you are real. The image is an abstraction, not real, but you are very real. So I run away from you in abstraction. And then I get hurt because you look at someone else. So, now I say to myself, "why am I doing all this?" Why is thought doing all this?—creating the image, adding to the image, taking things away from the image, and asking the question, "why is it doing it?"—and who is going to answer it? Is thought going to answer it?

Questioner: Thought cannot give the answer. We must see this.

KRISHNAMURTI: If you understand it, what takes place?

Questioner: Then there's silence.

KRISHNAMURTI: Don't use that word "silence." Just look at what takes place—which means that you have no image. That's what is taking place. When thought says, I have built it and I am going to find out why I have built it, and sees the absurdity of such a question, then all *image-making ceases!* Right? Are you doing it? Then I can look at you—my wife or husband—without an image. Follow this. Go into it a little more deeply. What takes place when there is no more image?

Questioner: There's no observer then.

KRISHNAMURTI: No Sir, go into it; don't reduce it. Go slowly Sir.

Questioner: There is real relationship.

KRISHNAMURTI: I don't know what that means! So far Sir, I've discovered only one thing: that thought has created the image and thought seeking to find an answer why, will create another image in which it will be caught. It's a vicious circle as long as thought is operating. Right? I have discovered that. Therefore thought is no longer creating an image. So what is my relationship—please follow this— what is my relationship to things, to people.

Questioner (1): Direct awareness, Sir.

Questioner (2): When thought ceases, the real me, the self, becomes in a way more apparent.

KRISHNAMURTI: Is there a real me without the thought? Sir, don't get caught in your own words, be careful.

Questioner: I see you as you are.

KRISHNAMURTI: No, no, I'm not concerned about you. What takes place, what is that relationship when I have no image about you?

Questioner: The dead person becomes a living thing. . . .

KRISHNAMURTI: Sir, I wish you would do this, actually: put away the images you have about me, or about your wife, or about somebody else and look. Then find out what that relationship is.

Questioner: (in French) If I am in relationship then I can follow the moods and thoughts of that person.

KRISHNAMURTI: That's not what I'm asking, if you don't mind. We are asking: "if I have no image about money,

about property, about you—my wife or husband or friend—
what is that relationship?"

Questioner: To ask this question is to be back in thought.

KRISHNAMURTI: No, no Madame, just look at it. I have no
image about you—and that's a tremendous thing I've discovered. Then I say to myself, "what is my relationship,
what is this relationship then, if I have no image?"

Questioner (1): This relationship ceases to be.

*Questioner (2): Sir, it's an extremely difficult question to
go into, because when we try to find out, put it into
words, then thought springs to action.*

KRISHNAMURTI: Look, Sir, let's make it very simple. You're
my friend, I have an image about you. Now, I have no
image about you. (Don't answer me Sir.) I have no image
about you. What has taken place in me? Not in my
relationship with you, what has actually taken place in me?
I want to know, what has actually taken place in me?

Questioner: Every second is new.

KRISHNAMURTI: Oh no. Please Madame, you're all guessing.
This isn't a guessing game.

Questioner: You're a fact, you're no longer an idea.

KRISHNAMURTI: Oh, no. You're not going into it. What has
taken place in me when I'm not creating an image about
everything? You don't even have time to examine and you
are ready to answer! Please, look at yourself. Find out what
happens if you have done this, if you're no longer an
image-making entity, what has taken place?

*Questioner: We cannot know because if we knew we
would conceptualize it. We still have the image!*

KRISHNAMURTI: Sir, I said, if you have no image at all—and we went through the whole process of making the image—if you don't do that any more, what takes place?

Questioner (1): The space where the image was is without the image.

Questioner (2): Sir, we seem to be one step behind, because we're not with you. Could we perhaps go back to the last step?

KRISHNAMURTI: The last step was, that thought which has created the image—through pleasure, through pain and all the rest of it—that thought is asking, "why am I doing this?"
And that thought says, I am doing it because—and therefore creates another image. Right? So, as long as thought is operating its function is to create images. We said, "I understand that, I've discovered that," so in the understanding of that, thought is in abeyance, quiet. Then I say to myself, what has taken place? When thought is completely quiet and not building an image about anything, what has taken place?

Questioner: (inaudible)

KRISHNAMURTI: Make it simple. Thought has been chasing its tail, over and over again. And thought says, "what a silly thing I'm doing," and stops. Right? Then what takes place?

Questioner: I cannot stop it, Sir.

KRISHNAMURTI: Then go on, chase the tail.

Questioner: Sir, then thought comes to an end, that's all we know now.

KRISHNAMURTI: I'm showing you Sir; if you do it yourself, it's very simple. Thought has been chasing its own tail.

Right? Now thought realizes how silly it is, therefore it stops! What takes place then? Please do it.

Questioner: At the moment when there is no image of you there is no image of myself.

KRISHNAMURTI: No, Sir. That is not the question I'm asking. When thought stops chasing its tail what takes place at that moment, at that second?

Questioner: We don't know.

KRISHNAMURTI: If you don't know, you haven't stopped chasing the tail.

Questioner: The thinker disappears.

KRISHNAMURTI: You see, you're all so eager to answer. You haven't really looked at yourself at all. You haven't spent a single minute looking at yourself. If you had, you would have inevitably come to this point, which is, that thought is chasing its own tail all the time. Then thought itself realizes how absurd this is and therefore it stops. Now, when it stops what takes place?

Questioner: We would be very still.

KRISHNAMURTI: How quick we are to answer, aren't we! Do we give up the game? That's what you're making it into, a guessing game. Look, Sir! Listen to this. When thought stops chewing its own tail endlessly, when it stops, what takes place?

Questioner: You are open to. . . .

KRISHNAMURTI: I am asking something which you're refusing to face. It is very simple; the moment thought stops chewing its own tail, you're full of energy—aren't you? Be-

213

cause in that chasing your energy has been dissipated. Right? Then you become very intense. No?

Questioner: (Inaudible)

KRISHNAMURTI: What happens to a mind that is very intense, not under tension, not under strain, but intense? What takes place? Have you ever been intense, about anything, have you? If you have what happens?

Questioner: Then you are not, as far as. . . .

KRISHNAMURTI: Wait, wait, Sir, you say something and dissipate it. When you are intense, what takes place? There's no problem, and therefore you are *not*. You are only when there's conflict.

Questioner: Then you're out of the door.

KRISHNAMURTI: You see, you're verbalizing. Don't do that Sir, please, we have gone into something very deep. If you would only go into it. In that intensity there is neither the observer nor the observed. Sir, when you love—go into it when you love, is there an observer? There is an observer only when love is desire and pleasure. When desire and pleasure are not associated with love, then love is intense— isn't it? It is something new every day because thought has not touched it.

5th August 1967

5

I THINK WE SHOULD be clear about why we have gathered here, and what is the intention of these dialogues. We said that they are not meant for mere intellectual amusement or exchange of opinions and ideas. What we want to do is something entirely different. In talking over together our problems we are exposing ourselves—not to anyone—but to ourselves so that we see things more clearly, and *seeing* as we said the other day is *acting*. And if we reduce this merely to a form of serious entertainment I'm afraid it will be of very little significance. So we will proceed with what we were talking about yesterday.

We were talking about knowing oneself, learning about oneself, and to learn about oneself one needs a great deal of humility. If you start by saying, "I know myself," you've already stopped learning about yourself. Or if you say, "there is nothing much to learn about myself because I know what I am—I'm a bundle of memories, ideas, experiences, tradition, a conditioned entity with innumerable contradictory reactions"—you've stopped learning about yourself. To learn about oneself requires considerable humility, never assuming that you know anything: that is, learning about oneself from the beginning and never accumulating. The moment you accumulate knowledge about yourself through your own discovery, that becomes the platform from which you begin to examine, learn, and therefore what you learn is merely further addition to what you already know. Humility is a state of mind that never acquires, never says, "I know." We were saying yesterday that there is this whole structure of the me, the self, with all its extraordinary complexity, and thought is the very basis of this structure which is the me. I think this morning it might be worthwhile to go into this question of what is thinking and what significance it has, and where thought has no significance at all: where thought must be exercised with care, with logic, with sanity, and where thought has very little meaning. Unless we know the two, we cannot possibly understand something much deeper, much more extensive, which thought cannot possibly touch. And that's what we are going to talk over together this morning. Shall we go into that?

In understanding thought we shall probably also discover what love is. I think the understanding of thought must inevitably lead to the other. So it is necessary to understand this whole complex structure of what thinking is, what memory is, how thought is conditioned and is always of the past and therefore never new. If we can grasp that perhaps we shall find out something—a state that is entirely different. So it seems to me that it is important to understand for ourselves what thinking is, how it originates, what is its beginning, how it conditions all action. And in understanding that, perhaps we shall be able to come upon something that thought has never discovered, which is that thought can never under any circumstances open the door. So let's go into it.

Why has thought become so important in the life of each one of us? Do please examine it for yourselves, go into yourself and find out. Thought being idea, thought which is the response of memory, thought which is the response of the accumulated memories in the brain cells—why do we give such extraordinary importance to ideas, which are organized thought? Perhaps many of us have not even asked such a question before. And if we have, we say, that's of very little importance, what is important is emotion, feelings. I don't see how you can separate the two. You may have a feeling, but if thought doesn't give it continuity that feeling dies very quickly. Do please observe this in yourself.

Why in our lives, in our daily grinding, boring, frightened lives, why has thought taken a place of such inordinate importance?

Questioner: We have made it so in order to protect ourselves.

KRISHNAMURTI: If I may suggest—I'm saying this courteously—please don't answer immediately, because if you do you stop yourself enquiring further. If you say, "thought has become so important because I have to protect myself," your enquiry is already finished. But if you began to enquire, being free from your opinions and conclusions, you would be free to go on to search, to ask, to flow.

Questioner: Thought is the only means we have of understanding ourselves or the Universe—anything at all.

KRISHNAMURTI: Is it? No, Sir. I have asked a question, I am asking myself the question, "why has thought become important in my life?" If you say, it is important "because," then you've already assumed something, you already have come to a conclusion and so your mind is no longer free to enquire, to look. I ask myself and I hope you are asking yourself: why has thought assumed such colossal importance? Intellectual ideas, theories, hypotheses, conclusions, ideas about God, the Universe, about what I should be, what I shouldn't be. Why has thought taken such predominant hold on my whole being?

217

Questioner: Is there a difference between "thinking" and "thought"?

KRISHNAMURTI: Surely all thought (whether thinking or thought) is the outcome of memory, isn't it? I think about my wife or my husband, about my family or my profession, which gives me a certain dignity, a certain prestige. I think about my wife or husband—we'll start with the most familiar. I think about her, which is an active present: I am thinking about her. The thinking about her is the response of my knowledge about her, my experience with her—sexual or whatever it is—and that is the memory I have about her. To think about her is a continuation of that memory. Right? Or, I have certain memories about her or him, and out of that memory there come certain responses, of pleasure, or pain; which also means I have thought about her in the past. Thinking and thought are similar; you can't divide it so neatly. Ask yourselves, as I am asking myself, why is one a slave to thought—thought, cunning, clever, thought that can organize; thought that can start things; thought that has invented so much; thought that has bred so many wars; thought that breeds such fear, such anxiety; thought that has enjoyed the pleasure of something yesterday, and gives to that pleasure a continuity in the present and also in the future—why is this thought always active, chattering, moving, constructing, taking away, adding, supposing?

Questioner: Sir, one thing about thought is that from the time we were small children we were encouraged to think. Nobody ever told us that there is something else, so thinking has become a habit.

KRISHNAMURTI: Yes, Sir, all right. There is not "something else," nobody has told you about something else. Forget the something else; I am asking, why have you given such importance to thought?

218

Questioner (1): One of the reasons is, thought allows us to get new pleasure, new enjoyment; it is the means by which we get pleasure.

Questioner (2): Sir, the moment we answer such a question we're giving importance to thought and therefore we cannot explore.

Questioner (3): We must have clarity; we think thought is the means to it.

KRISHNAMURTI: Somebody has put you this question: "why have you given such importance to thought?"; and they say to you "you must answer it and the answer must be right, not just guesswork, otherwise you'll be shot tomorrow morning!" How will you answer it?

Questioner: Can we live without thinking?

KRISHNAMURTI: I really don't know. Let us take one thing and go through with it. Perhaps we shall be able to understand a very simple thing. I had a certain desire yesterday and I've fulfilled it, and in the very fulfilling of it there was a certain pleasure, a certain gratification. And thought comes along and says, "how very nice that was, I must have more of it." What has taken place? There is a desire, which has been fulfilled, and out of that fulfilment there is a certain pleasure, enjoyment. Then what takes place? You tell me.

Questioner: You want to repeat it.

KRISHNAMURTI: Who wants it repeated?

Questioner: The experiencer.

KRISHNAMURTI: Who is the experiencer? Do look at it, Sir. Go into it. Who is the experiencer who says, "yesterday I had a marvellous experience and I must have more of it"?

219

Questioner (1): Memory.

Questioner (2): *Thought itself. . . . the experience is the experiencer.*

KRISHNAMURTI: Quite right, that's so simple, isn't it? It is said, thought itself is the experiencer. That is, there was an experience yesterday which was pleasurable, a great delight, and that delight has left a mark on the mind as memory. Then out of that memory comes thought and says, I must have more of it. So thought is the experiencer. It's so simple—isn't it? No?

Questioner: Who is the experiencer in the first experience?

KRISHNAMURTI: Ah, the first experience, the very first—is there an experiencer? What do you say Sirs, are you all going to sleep or am I asleep?

Questioner: Sir, it seems to me there was an experiencer who said that you had a desire yesterday and it was gratified. So, the one who had the desire and was gratified, that was the experiencer.

KRISHNAMURTI: That's so simple, Sir. What are we discussing? It's so clear, isn't it? If there was no memory at all and therefore there was only desire, fulfilment, pleasure, it would finish there! But the experiencer wants that pleasure to continue, which is thought. Right? So I see thought sustains a pleasure. Thought gives continuity to a pleasure that I had yesterday. And thought gives continuity to the other form of pleasure which is pain, which is fear. Which means: thought as the experiencer says, "I must have that pleasure repeated tomorrow"—the sexual—any form of pleasure. And thought also gives nourishment, continuity to fear, by thinking about it. So the experiencer, which means the thinker, is both the pleasure and the pain; both the entity that gives nourishment to pleasure and to fear. So when thought demands a continuity to pleasure, it is also constantly inviting fear!

Questioner: Is it possible to die to that thinker and to that memory?

KRISHNAMURTI: I don't know, we are going to find out.

Questioner: Can we understand desire, which makes thought?

KRISHNAMURTI: Sir, have you observed your desire, how it comes into being? Haven't you noticed it?

Questioner: You see a thing and you want it.

KRISHNAMURTI: Now why do you want it? You see something, "you want it" you say, but how does this want arise?

Questioner: It attracts you.

KRISHNAMURTI: What do you mean by that word? Sir, be simple about it, you will see it in a second for yourself.

Questioner: Desire arises from the pleasure we get out of something.

KRISHNAMURTI: Not "out of something," Sir. You see a beautiful house, a beautiful woman, a handsome man, and so on and so on—seeing comes first, right? Then there is sensation, contact, and out of this comes desire—doesn't it? I see you—very intelligent, alive, active—that gives me a feeling of envy, which is a form of desire—to be like you, or to surpass you. So, it's fairly simple to see how desire arises. When I see a beautiful car, I touch it, I see the lines, the power, and so on—it gives a sensation. I want that sensation to be fulfilled, I want to own it. The "I" is the thinker who says, "how nice it would be to get into that car and drive!" Right? That is so clear, if one can be simple about it. So there it is. The thinker is both the giver of pain, pleasure and fear, and what we want is the continuation of pleasure without fear. And that's what each one of us is seeking: pleasure, in the wife or the husband, pleasure in the family, pleasure which one derives from this absurd thing called "nationality," the pleasures of finding through thought a so-called God, and so on. And the other side of the coin is the avoidance of pain and the avoidance of fear.

Questioner: Is not desire also wanting to give, to help and to serve?

KRISHNAMURTI: I wonder why we want to serve? The petrol station says, "we give you awfully good service." (Laughter) Don't laugh, please, I'm not being sarcastic, Madame, I'm just observing, trying to understand that word "service," "help," "give." What does it all mean? Does a flower full of beauty, light and loveliness, say to itself, "I am giving, helping, serving"? It *is!* And because it is not trying to do anything it covers the earth. So, let us go into this. Thought as the thinker separates pain from pleasure. Follow this, watch it in yourself. When it says, I must have pleasure, it doesn't see that in this very demand it is inviting fear. And thought in our human relationship —not in the laboratory or in some technological activity— is always demanding pleasure, which it covers by different words like "service," "loyalty," "helping," "giving," "sustaining" you know, all those words. I wonder why you give importance to the family? Would you tell me?

Questioner: Because we are afraid of loneliness.

KRISHNAMURTI: All right. You are afraid to be lonely, therefore you give importance to the family and you say out of that fear of loneliness, "I love my family"—right? And is that love?

Questioner: That's self-protection.

KRISHNAMURTI: I don't know what it is, I'm just asking you. Thought is so cunning, so clever, that it covers up everything for its own convenience. I am afraid, lonely, miserable—and the family becomes extraordinarily important because it covers my loneliness, my misery. So I see (perhaps you don't) that thought in its demand for pleasure—which brings bondage—also breeds fear, which has its own bondage. This is what always takes place in our relationships with each other. This is not being cynical or bitter, this is actually what goes on. And so what happens? Thought is the breeder of this duality. Right? That is, I'm violent; there's violence which gives me great pleasure and also there is the desire for peace, to be kind, to be gentle. Thought engenders both—right? One sees that, understands that. And one asks oneself: "but thought has a certain importance?" Thought has importance—thought as memory or rather the accumulated memory from which thought arises and thought has built this memory, given life to this memory. By thinking about the pleasure which I had yesterday, the pleasure which is dead, which is a memory, I am giving to that dead memory a new life. Please watch this in yourself. Thought is reviving the dead past, the dead pleasure, the dead memory, and from that very dead memory thought has come into being. This is what is going on all our life. So thought not only breeds this contradiction in our lives—as pleasure and fear—but also thought has accumulated the memory of the innumerable pleasures we have had and from those memories thought is reborn. So thought is always the past! Thought is always the old!

Questioner: But in this thought, revived by memory and sustaining memory, is there never anything new? Is it always the same material?—always just that?

KRISHNAMURTI: Sir, don't answer "no." Look at it. You have a new experience—if there is such a thing—which we'll go into. You have a new feeling, a new intensity, "elan," then what takes place? Do watch, don't answer me.

223

Please be good enough to answer yourself, not me. You had a new experience yesterday; you say it is new and you call it an experience. Is it new? If you are able to recognize it as an experience, is it new? You understand? If I recognize something—you or an experience—that recognition is the outcome of something which I've already known, otherwise I cannot recognize it! So thought however cunning it may be, however subtle, however devious it may be, thought is always the old. Right?

Questioner: Sir, do you mean that if a new experience occurs and we do not recognize it, then we are unconscious?

KRISHNAMURTI: No, you wouldn't call it an experience at all.

Questioner: If we're conscious of it, surely we call it an experience?

KRISHNAMURTI: You do?

Questioner: For us, experience and consciousness are synonymous words.

KRISHNAMURTI: Yes Sir, quite right, but if you do not recognize that experience you have no experience.

Questioner: Well, by that you mean that we're unconscious of it, just as if we were asleep?

KRISHNAMURTI: Yes, all right, if you like to put it that way.

Questioner: It happens, you don't even know. . . .

KRISHNAMURTI: You know it, that's quite right.

Questioner: Do you mean that no matter how unprecedented something may seem it's never new, as far as we're concerned? I go to some country which I've never seen before, know nothing about it, like Central Africa, and there I see something strange and unprecedented. I see it. Do you mean that. . . .

KRISHNAMURTI: Wait, Sir; you see it, what takes place?

Questioner: I say: how extraordinary I never saw this before, so therefore. . . .

KRISHNAMURTI: Go on Sir, go on into it; "never saw it before," then what takes place?

Questioner: I try to relate it to some category. . . .

KRISHNAMURTI: Yes.

Questioner: . . . . That makes it so I can think of what its place is in proper proportion, and therefore I immediately make it old.

KRISHNAMURTI: Therefore, what has happened? You see something new and translate it in terms of the old. The moment your thought interferes with it as the "thinker" you've reduced it to the old.

Questioner: Then one can see something new, but the thinker makes it old.

KRISHNAMURTI: Quite right! The moment the thinker interferes with it, it has become the old.

Questioner: Yes Sir, I can see that.

KRISHNAMURTI: That's all. Now, let's proceed a little bit further. Thought has importance. Right? Otherwise I couldn't get from this place, from this tent, to the place where I live. I couldn't go to the office, I couldn't function there; the very language which one uses is the result of

225

thought, and so on. Thought has vital importance. But, has thought any importance in relation to that thing which we call Love?

Questioner: But we don't know what love is.

KRISHNAMURTI: We're going to find out what love is; or, what love is not. We said love is not desire. I don't know why, somebody has said it. Somebody has said, love is not pleasure. The speaker has said it and we're going to find out why. Why is love not desire? What do you think?

Questioner: Desire is memory.

KRISHNAMURTI: No Sir, don't you see, the moment you have said "desire is memory," you have stopped. I love my wife—God knows why—but I say, I love my wife. What does that mean? In that love desire is involved—sexual pleasure, the pleasure of having somebody in the house to look after the children, to cook, to worry about all that while I'm at the office, and so on. And when the wife looks at somebody else or doesn't give me complete satisfaction —sexually, or in different ways—I get annoyed or jealous. No? You're all very silent.

Questioner: But at least at the beginning there was something different. (laughter)

KRISHNAMURTI: He is betraying himself! (laughter) Excuse me! The questioner says, "it was different at the beginning." Naturally! That question needn't be answered, need it? (laughter) Now just go back to it. I consider that I love my wife. I say, I love my wife or husband or family. What is involved in that? There is desire, there is pleasure, there is fear, there is anxiety; there is a sense of escaping from myself, from my loneliness, through the family. All that I cover by this word "love." Right? And that is an accepted morality. That's legally acceptable to the culture, to the society in which we live. What we call love is hedged

226

about; in it there is jealousy, envy, greed, fear, bullying, domination—and occasional joy. Is that love? I don't say, it is not; I don't know. That is what we live with, that's what we call love, that is the thing that is important to us.

Questioner: It can be with great affection.

KRISHNAMURTI: Of course. So I'm asking myself, what has thought done? You understand? When I first met her, my wife, I said, I love this woman, we're going to marry, have sex, pleasure, companionship. But gradually boredom comes with her, with the routine, boredom with sex; and she also gets bored with the whole thing. But there are children. And she looks at somebody else—because after all we all want excitement—and I begin to be tortured by jealousy, by hate. You all know this, don't you?

Questioner: Sir, you are analyzing something very delicate with a blunt instrument; it is not quite as brutal as that.

KRISHNATURI: Of course not. There is tenderness, there is care, there is so-called responsibility, insurance, the pride of a clever son who is climbing the ladder, and so on. It isn't just one thing, it is *everything*—tenderness, affection, jealousy, hate, fear, loneliness—all that is covered by that word "love." No?

Questioner: I think there is another sort of love: when one wants someone to be happy.

KRISHNAMURTI: If one had a different kind of love, everything would be perfect! Obviously! But, I haven't got it! Sir, I'm going to find out. I say to myself: I see now that where there is desire and pleasure with all its pain—all that we described previously—obviously that's not love. And thought—please follow this—thought which has given continuity to pleasure, thought which has given continuity to fear, is not love. So thought is not love! Right?

227

Questioner: Is thought a creative power?

KRISHNAMURTI: Sir, I don't know what these two words mean, "creative" and "power." That's not what we are discussing for the moment. We are trying to find out what that quality of love is in which there is no fear, in which there is no pleasure. If you do not want fear in love, you must also put away pleasure, because fear and pleasure are the two sides of the same coin. So thought, which gives a continuity to desire as pleasure, must also give a continuity to fear—fear of my wife and the pleasure of my wife, or my husband, and so on. Thought cannot possibly bring about what love is. Right?

Questioner: Thought can only create an image about love.

KRISHNAMURTI: Sir, it has no meaning. An image, a symbol hanging in a church has no meaning. So please follow this next question. Can I live in this world with my wife, with my family, without desire, pleasure and fear? If I have that desire, pleasure and fear, it would be dishonest on my part to use the word "love." Do you swallow this pill? So I begin to ask, is it possible for thought, in relationship, never to interfere? Because when thought interferes it will bring about in that relationship desire, pleasure and fear. Please follow this to the end. Is it possible for thought not to interfere at all?

Questioner: If we give up every desire there will be no thought.

KRISHNAMURTI: Sir, that's just a supposition. Look, I have a husband or wife and there is this agony going on between us—fear, desire, pleasure, anxiety—all that I call "love." And I say, what a monstrous way of living! What a brutal existence it is! And I ask myself, is it possible for thought not to enter into this relationship at all? Which means— follow it carefully—that I don't chew over the sexual pleasure that I had yesterday, that there will be no question of domination either by me or by her—domination being "aggression," whether sexual or in any other form— and that I am completely free and so is she! Because if I depend on her for my pleasure I'm a slave to her. Can I live with her without thought creating all these contradictory states with their efforts and endless quarrels in myself? If I can, then perhaps—*perhaps*—I will know what it is to love. Unfortunately the churches throughout the world, temples and mosques, have divided this love into the profane and the sacred. But I don't even know how to love a tree, let alone my wife and my neighbor—I'm willing to destroy him in business.

So, I see now how thought operates. I have watched thought building this house brick by brick: thought which has built this house and is caught in it. And we're saying, how are we to get out? How are we to break down the walls which thought has created? And the questioner is the thought itself! Right?

Questioner: Why should thought ask, "what is love?"

KRISHNAMURTI: It generally doesn't ask, because it's too frightened to enquire. It may break up the family, you may never go back to the temple. If you ask that question it is a terribly disturbing question, so we avoid it; and we lead a respectable bourgeois life with pleasure, with desire, with fear and all the rest of it.

Questioner: When you see what thought is doing, why do you continue it?

KRISHNAMURTI: But does one see what thought is doing? Do you—actually Sir, not only you but each one of us— actually see how thought builds this house in which it is caught? Or is it just an idea which you have heard and repeated and therefore it has become a theory, something which you have concluded? You understand Sir? If I want to find out the quality of what may be called love, in which there is no fear at all and therefore no pleasure, then

229

I have to shatter the whole house which I have built—my family, my responsibility, or the other form which is to run away from the family and say, "I'm not responsible!" This is a tremendous problem. Unless you solve this I don't see how you can go a step further. You can go on theoretically; you can discuss endlessly whether there is a God or not, what a particular Savior was, or was not—all that. But if you really, deeply inside yourself, want to go a step further, this has got to be settled. Because unless you have love you have no beauty, and without beauty and love you can never find out what truth is. Not, "truth is in everything"—there is truth in finding out how thought operates, what desire is, what pleasure is, what fear is. But if the mind wants to go very deeply and widely this question of love has to be understood. And love is not sentiment, it is not devotion, it is not service—it is none of those things! It is only when thought has understood itself and is quiet—never interfering—then it's something—then you are in a different dimension altogether. You hear all this but what you hear is not "what is"—the word is never the thing. What one can do is only to go into this question of thought and be constantly aware of this problem of desire, pleasure and fear. You can't escape from it. You have to understand it, look at it, live with it, be aware of it, conscious of it.

Questioner: Sir, thought enters in relationship; but how may it come about that love does, which is not born out of memory?

KRISHNAMURTI: It happens only when your whole being, everything in you says, I must find out what love is; when you give all your attention, Sir, to find out. You understand? Then thought begins to wither away. But if you're not interested in it, if you're not as hungry to find out as you are for food, then thought dominates, destroys everything that it touches in this relationship.

Questioner: Then love will be full of energy, or not?

KRISHNAMURTI: Find out, Sir. The energy that thought—and thought is energy—wastes in desire, in pain, fear, anxiety—when all that is gone then there is only energy—which is love. But you see, I really dislike to use that word because it has been so corrupted. Every man and woman talks about love, all the magazines, newspapers, every missionary, every priest in every church talks everlastingly about love of God! That's not love at all. Love is something that thought cannot possibly come upon and we are so full of thought; thought can never come upon that beauty, that ecstasy.

6th August 1967

6

THIS IS THE LAST discussion or dialogue. We have talked during these past five days about various forms of violence, self-knowing and the processes of thought. So what shall we talk about this morning?

Questioner: *Sir, it seems to me we have forgotten to consider another aspect of our intelligence. Thought can combine in different ways material from our past and therefore bring about something which is apparently new and generally called invention.*

KRISHNAMURTI: I understand. I think we have much more important things to discuss, talk about, than merely invention.

Questioner: *Sir, you said when there are no thoughts there is energy. There are many ideas about energy. Is it possible to speak about energy?*

KRISHNAMURTI: Is it possible to talk about that energy which comes into being, which is part of thought, when thought doesn't bring about a contradiction in itself?

Questioner: Sir, you talked about two kinds of ideas, technical ideas which we are not talking about here, and the ideas created by thought. But aren't there ideas beyond the human mind in the universe?

KRISHNAMURTI: I think it would be much more worthwhile this morning if we could spend some time talking over together the question of awareness, attention and meditation. We shall perhaps answer some of these questions that have just been put this morning. We'll begin by enquiring into ourselves and finding out what we mean by awareness. Because it seems to me most of us are not aware, not only of what we are talking about, but aware of our feelings, aware of our environment, aware of the colors around us, the people, the kind of cars that we pass by on the road, the shape of the trees, the clouds, the movement of the water. To see the birds—and perhaps some of you saw this morning, very early, long before the sun rose, how extraordinarily clear it was—the air was perfumed. We're not aware of the outside things at all. Perhaps it is because we are so concerned with ourselves, with our problems, with our ideas, with our own pleasures, pursuits and ambitions, that we are not aware, outside, objectively. And yet we talk a great deal about "being aware."

Once the speaker was traveling with some people in a car, there was a chauffeur driving and I was sitting beside him. There were three gentlemen behind discussing awareness very intently and asking me questions about awareness. Unfortunately at that moment the driver was looking somewhere else and ran over a goat—the three gentlemen were still discussing awareness (laughter)—and yet were totally unaware, unconscious, that they had run over a goat. And the chauffeur was not in the least concerned. When we pointed out this lack of attention, or awareness, on the part of the people who were trying to be

233

aware, it was a total surprise to them. And it is the same with most of us. We are not aware either of outward things or of inward things. So may we this morning spend some time talking about this awareness?

Most of our minds are rather dull, insensitive, because we are unhealthy, we've had problems with which we have lived for days together, months, years—the problem of children, marriage, earning a livelihood, the brutal society in which we live—all that has made us insensitive, dull, our reactions are rather slow. Such a mind attempts to be aware, hoping thereby somehow to go beyond the limitations which society, the individual and so on, have placed upon it. In talking about awareness I think it is important to understand how very simple it is; not to complicate it, not to say, "it must be this," "it must not be that," but to begin very, very simply because it's a tremendously complex problem. We must begin very simply, go into it step by step, not analytically, but observing ourselves as we are and being aware of what we are, and from there move step by step. Can we do that this morning, just for the fun of it? I think that will sharpen the mind, because we are rather crude people, assertive, aggressive, self-important, wanting to tell others what we think, what they should do, what they should not do. We want to boss others, we assume responsibility which is none of ours. So we live in a kind of self-important, self-projecting world of our own, and living in that, we talk about awareness as being something extraordinarily mysterious.

So, if we may this morning discuss or talk over together a problem which is very interesting, and also if we could go into it very deeply, we will take a journey without end. Shall we do that? Don't agree with me please. See for yourself if it is important or not. Because I feel if we can understand this very simple thing we shall be able to understand the structure of our own mind, the states of various levels of our own being—where there is contradiction, where there is blindness, where there is self-assertiveness, brutality; we shall then become aware of all the boiling, burning things in us. So let's begin.

234

First of all don't let us define what awareness is. Because if we do, each one of us will give it a different meaning, a different definition; but we shall find out what awareness means as we go along. The moment you define what awareness is, you've already blocked yourself by words, by a conclusion. But if you say, I'm going to find out what it means, then your mind becomes supple, elastic, and you can go along. So let's go into it. Don't complicate it, because as we begin to look into awareness it will become more and more complex, but if you start with the complexity of it you won't be able to see its extraordinary simplicity, and therefore through the very simplicity discover the diversity and the contradictoriness and the dissimilarity that exists in this awareness. Am I making it complex?

Questioner: You mentioned awareness about things and states of mind. Does that mean that awareness always has an object, such as fear?

KRISHNAMURTI: We're going to find out. We're going to begin. Look! I know nothing about it. Right? I know nothing about awareness. I'm going to find out what it means, not what somebody tells me. First of all am I aware, conscious, of outward things?—the shape of the tree, the bird sitting on the telegraph pole preening itself, the pot-holes in the road, the face opposite me. That is, just to look—to see! Or, do I see the image that I have about that bird, or that tree, or the image which I have about the face I see in front of me? Right? That is, not only do I see the bird on the post—I also have an image of that bird—so there is the *seeing* and the image which sees the bird. Is that somewhat clear? I see you—actually, visually—and I also have an image about you—you're old, young, nice looking, or you're dirty, you're this, you're that. Right?

Questioner: How are we ever sure that we are seeing a bird without an image?

235

KRISHNAMURTI: Sir, look. Forget the bird. You're sitting there and I'm sitting here. How do you know that you see me? How do I know that I see you?—you're there and I'm here.

Questioner: Sir, there is something that is not clear to me. Do I see the bird or the image of it?—I can't understand.

KRISHNAMURTI: This is a conundrum! Let's forget the bird, let's forget the tree, let's forget everything. There you are. You're sitting there and the speaker is sitting on the platform. You see him, not only actually (brown coat, etc.) but also you see him through the image you have about him. Right? I see you not only visually, what you actually look like, but also, because I have known you, I have an image about you. Now that's part of awareness, isn't it? I'm aware of your face, your color, the scarf around your neck, the brown shirt—but I also have an image about you because I have known you—you have said pleasant or unpleasant things—I have built an image about you. That's part of awareness isn't it? Right? Of course!

Now, go a step further. I see you through the image which I have built about you. I see you—not only the brown shirt and so on—but also I see you through my image. Right? So actually I don't see you at all! That's part of awareness, isn't it? To realize that the image which is looking at you prevents the mind from looking at you directly. This is fairly simple. No? That's also part of awareness isn't it? I am aware of the brown shirt you have and the color of the scarf around your neck. I'm also aware that I have an image about you and that image is looking at you. That's part of awareness. Obviously, Sirs.

Now, next move. By being aware of this, that awareness says, I am really not looking at you at all—my image is looking at you! Are you following this? My image is looking at you. First of all I am aware that I have an image, which I was not aware of before. Then I am aware

236

how that image has come into being. Right? Now *how* has that image come into being? That image has come into being because you have hurt me, or you have said pleasant things to me, you have flattered me, you have said, "what a marvelous person you are," or "for God's sake become more intelligent," or this or that. Through your verbal expression and the feeling which you have put into those words, and my reactions to those words and to those feelings, I have built an image about you—which is the memory that I have about you. Right?

Questioner: But you form an image about someone even the first time you meet. . . .

KRISHNAMURTI: Yes, yes. It can be in an instant. I don't like your face, or I like your face. I like the perfume which you have on, I don't like it, and so on. I've already built an image, instantly. Right? So I am aware for the first time that I have an image about you. And also I am aware that this image has been put together by like and dislike. I am a German and you are a Frenchman and I don't like you and so on. So I am aware through the image I have built about you, from my reactions to you. Right? Shall we go on? Are you following the words or actually watching yourselves, watching the image you have about me or about somebody else, how that image has been built? If you have a husband or a wife you know very well how that image has been built; and are you aware of this image? Not, whether you like it or dislike it. Because if you are aware and say "I like" or "I don't like" then you are adding to that image. Right? Or you say, I must get rid of that image. You're again adding to that image. But if you observe without any reaction to the image—I wonder if you're following all this, is it too difficult?—would you like to "take a trip"?

This is a very complex process. Unless you follow this very, very closely you're going to miss the whole thing. Therefore you have to pay attention. I am aware of your brown shirt and scarf and the color of the scarf. I am also aware that I look at you through the image I have built about you and the image has been built through your words, through your gestures, or through my prejudice about you or my like and dislike of you. That is part of awareness. And also I see I am aware that this image prevents me from looking at you *directly!* It prevents me from looking at you, coming into contact with you directly. Then I say to myself, "I must get rid of this image." You're following this? Then begins the conflict, doesn't it? When I want to get rid of the image which I have built about you, to be free of it, because I want to come closer into contact with you, to see you directly, that is another form of reaction to the image.

I said, I am aware that I have the image which prevents me from looking, from observing exactly *what is*, what exactly you are or exactly I am. So I want to get rid of it, I want to be free of it because this might be more profitable, it might be more pleasurable, or it might bring me some kind of a deeper, wider experience. And all this is part of awareness. The moment I want to get rid of that image, I have entered a battle with the image which is conflict. So I am aware what has happened now. I am aware of your brown shirt and the color of the scarf, I am aware of the image that I have built about you. I am aware that this image is preventing me from coming directly in touch with you, seeing exactly what you are, or that the image which I have about myself prevents me from looking at myself. I want to get rid of that image because I've heard you say, self-knowledge is very important. Therefore I don't want to have an image about myself; I want to get rid of it. And when I want to get rid of it, then there is a conflict between the former image and a new image which I have created. You're following all this? So I am now in conflict. And if it is a pleasurable conflict I want it to go on. If the conflict promises a certain pleasure at the end of it, I want it to go on. And if that conflict breeds pain I want to get rid of that pain. So I am aware of the whole pattern of what is taking place. Right? I hope you are doing this with me—taking your own image which you have about somebody, looking at it, being aware of it, as you are aware of the tent, the limitations of the tent, the curve of the tent, the structure of the tent, the patches in the tent, the holes, and so on. Similarly you are aware of yourself with our image and what is implied by it. Now I'm in conflict. Either I am aware of that conflict as it is, or I want to alter that conflict into something which will give me more; or I am in conflict very superficially, just on the surface; or, I am aware of the deeper layers of this conflict. So awareness is not merely a superficial observance of conflicts within myself, but also through this awareness the deeper conflicts are being opened up. Right? If the deeper layers of conflicts are opened up by being aware, then if there is fear in that, I want to shut them all up, I don't want to look. So I run away from them: run away from them through drink, drugs, women, men, amusement, entertainment, churches—all the rest of it. All that is part of awareness, isn't it?—the running away from fear, and giving importance to the things I have run to.

I am aware that I am lonely, miserable. I don't know a way out of it, or if I do know a way out it's too difficult; therefore I run away—run away to church, to drugs, to Communism, to every form of entertainment. And because I have run away from the thing of which I am afraid, to something which helps me to escape, those things become tremendously important. Right? So I'm attached to those things. It may be a wife, a family—whatever it is. Now all that is part of awareness, isn't it? I've begun very slowly—step by step—I watched your shirt, the color of your shirt, the color of your scarf, and gone deeper and deeper until I found that I have a whole network of escapes. I haven't searched them out, I haven't analyzed them; by being aware I have begun to penetrate deeper and deeper and deeper. Right? Are you following all this?

Questioner: I don't follow. I see about being aware. . . . but then comes a little jump about inner escapes. Could you please go over it again?

KRISHNAMURTI: What is the jump?

Questioner: Between awareness and our escape, from for instance, inner loneliness.

KRISHNAMURTI: Oh, I thought I had made it clear. I have built an image about you and I was never aware of that image; and I become aware of it by observing outer things, by being aware of external things. Naturally from the external things I move to inner things. And there I discover I have an image about you. I went into it, that's clear, isn't it? Now, by becoming aware of that image I find that I have built it in order to protect myself; or I have built it because you have said such brutal things to me that they remain in my memory, or you have said pleasant things which again remain in my memory. So there is the image which I have built, and I realize this image prevents me from looking deeper into my relationship with you. Right?

Questioner: You mean, Sir, that this awareness that you have is not just limited to one person but in every field. . . ?

KRISHNAMURTI: Of course, of course I have images about everything—about you, about my wife, about my children, about my country, about God. (Sound of jet overhead) Were you aware of the noise of that jet—were you aware of it? Were you aware of your reaction to it? And the reaction was: I wish it would go away because I want to find out, I want him to talk more, it's preventing me from listening. Or did you just listen to that extraordinary thunder? When you listened to that thunder without any choice you listened entirely differently, didn't you? No? You followed the thunder as it went further and further away. You listened to it and then you became aware of the different sounds of the river—didn't you?—of those children far away? But if you said, I don't like that sound because I want to listen here, I want to find out, then what has happened? Then you're in conflict, aren't you? You want to listen and you're

240

prevented by that noise, so there is resistance between the noise and the desire to listen, to find out; therefore there was conflict, and you were lost in that conflict. You neither listened to the thunder nor listened to what was being said. So let's proceed.

I have built an image about you, and I have several other images—perhaps dozens of them—and I see, I realize. I am aware that this image prevents me from looking at you more clearly; and I want to get rid of that image because I want to see you more clearly, understand you directly. This image prevents me, therefore I want to get rid of it; hence a conflict, because I want to understand you better. So there is a conflict—follow this—a conflict between the original image which I have about you and the new image which I have in mind, which is to look at you. Right? So there is conflict between the two. And as I don't know how to get rid of both these images I get tired, I get weary and as I have no way of solving this, the old image and the new image and the conflict between them, I escape—and I have a network of escapes, of which I am slowly becoming aware: drink, smoking, the incessant chatter, the offering of opinions, judgments, evaluations—dozens of escapes. I'm aware of superficial escapes and as I watch, as I am aware of these superficial escapes, I'm also beginning to discover the deeper layers of escapes. Are you following all this?

Questioner: In doing so I lose touch with the observed.

KRISHNAMURTI: I'm coming to that Sir. You see you are not actually doing it. If you are doing it step by step you will soon discover the nature of the observer. So what has happened? Awareness has exposed a network of escapes—superficial escapes—and also with that awareness I see a deeper level of escapes—the motives, the traditions, the fears which I have and so on. So there I am. Beginning with the brown shirt and the scarf I have discovered—awareness has shown—this extraordinary complex entity that I am—actually shown it!—not theoretically. You're following, Sir? That is, this awareness has actually shown *what is!* Until now the observer has been watching all this taking place. I have watched that shirt, the color of the scarf, as though it were something outside me—which it is—right? Then I have watched the image which I have built about you. Then that awareness has shown the complexity of this image and I'm still the observer of this image. So there is the image and the observer of that image. (I am working and you are not!) So again there is the duality: the observer and the thing observed which is the image; and the dozens of images which I have (if I have them) and the escapes from the various forms of conflict which these images have caused, superficially and deeply. And there is still the observer watching them.

Now, that awareness again goes on, deeper. Who is the observer? Is the observer different from the images? Is not the observer another image? So one image, as the observer, observes the several images round him or in him. No? This observer is really the censor, the person who says "I like," "I don't like," "I like this image so I'm going to keep it," "the other image I don't like so I want to get rid of it." But the observer is put together by the various images which have come into being through the reactions to the various images. Are you following all this?

Questioner: But all images are in the observer.

KRISHNAMURTI: Of course, of course.

Questioner: They are not separated.

KRISHNAMURTI: Perfectly right.

Questioner: But you say it is an image that sees another image.

KRISHNAMURTI: Of course. I examined, I explored it, until I came to the point where I said the observer is also the image, only he has separated himself and observes. Sir, please, this requires a great deal of real *looking*, not accepting anything that anybody says. This observer has come into being through the memories of various images and their reactions. So the observer separates himself from the other images and then says, "how am I to get rid of these images?" So this image is a permanent image! And this permanent image which thinks it is permanent says, I want to get rid of all the other images because they are really the cause of trouble, they really bring conflict, so it puts the blame on the other images. Whereas the observer who is the image, he is the central cause of all this mischief.

Questioner: The image must get rid of itself.

KRISHNAMURTI: Who is the entity that is going to get rid of it? Another image! It is really very important to understand this.

Questioner: Sir, if we look at these images we see they are made of thought. If we look at the image of ourself, the observer, we see that it is he that builds up in the same way. . . . I've got to this point.

KRISHNAMURTI: Yes Sir, you're perfectly right. We've got to that point. This awareness has revealed that there is a central image put together by the various other images, which has taken precedence; it is the censor, the evaluator, the judge, and it says, "I must get rid of all those others." So between him and the others there is a conflict. Right Sir? And we keep up this conflict all the time, and because we don't know how to resolve this conflict we have further escapes. Either through neurosis or through conscious, deliberate escapes—drink, church, whatever it is. As this awareness pushes itself deeper—not you push it—you ask: is the observer different from the other images? The other images are the result of judgments, of opinions, conclusions, hurts, nationality—so the observer is the result of all the other images.

Questioner: We are afraid of such complexity. . . .

KRISHNAMURTI: But life is that! Therefore you are afraid of life, therefore you escape from life. You see, you're not really paying complete attention to this, and that's why it's so difficult to talk "against" something. Look Sir, I have an image about you. That image has been put together by hurt, by like and dislike—that's a fact. That like and dislike has created another image in me—hasn't it?—not only the image about you but the other image, that I must not like or dislike; because it is absurd to like and dislike. Therefore I have built an image which says, "I must not like or dislike," which is the outcome of building an image and seeing what is implied in it; this brings the other image into being.

Questioner: Some minds don't work that way at all.

KRISHNAMURTI: I don't know how some minds work.

Questioner: Well mine doesn't.

KRISHNAMURTI: All right. We're talking about awareness, not how your mind works or my mind works.

Questioner: Supposing you don't create images?

KRISHNAMURTI: There's no question of "supposing."

Questioner: But I don't.

KRISHNAMURTI: What do you mean "suppose"?

Questioner: I'm not supposing, if I feel it is a fact.

KRISHNAMURTI: What is a fact? If you say, "I'm a stupid person," won't it hurt you? Or hurt me?

Questioner: Why should it?

KRISHNAMURTI: "Why should it," and being hurt, are two different things.

Questioner: *It won't, it won't hurt.*

KRISHNAMURTI: All right, it won't hurt, I'm very glad. You see how we go off on something very trivial.

So the observer is the observed. You understand Sirs? There is the image of the observer; between the observer and the various images he has around him, there is a division, there is a separation, a time interval, and hence he wants to conquer them, he wants to subjugate them, he wants to destroy them; he wants to get rid of them and hence there is a conflict between the observer and the observed. Right? And he says, "as long as I have conflict I must be in confusion." So he says, "I must get rid of this conflict." The very desire to get rid of that conflict creates another image. Follow all this Sir, very closely. Awareness has revealed all this, which is to reveal the various states of my mind, reveal various images, the contradictoriness between the images, the conflict, the despair of not being able to do anything about it, the escapes, the neurotic assumptions and so on. All that has been revealed through cautious, hesitant awareness; and there is an awareness that the observer is the observed. Please follow this! Not a superior entity is aware that the observer is the observed, but this awareness has revealed the observer as the observed. Not who is aware! Are you following all this? You know this is real meditation.

Now we can proceed. Now what takes place when the observer realizes that he is the observed? He has realized it not through any form of intellectual concept, idea, opinion, enforcement; he has realized this whole structure through this awareness—by being aware of the color of the shirt, the scarf, and moving, moving, deeper and deeper.

Questioner (1): *Sir, I am extremely sorry to interrupt but there's an important question that I don't understand and that is, you say awareness sees that the observer is the observed. Now, does that mean that he is the actual observed or the reaction to the observed?*

KRISHNAMURTI: I don't quite understand your question, Sir.

Questioner (1): Well, you say that the observer is the observed.

KRISHNAMURTI: I don't say it.

Questioner (1): All right, awareness discovers that. You said that.

KRISHNAMURTI: I did.

Questioner (1): So, here I have an image of you, let's say, and then awareness discovers that I am that observed, the observed is the image. Do you mean that the observer is the image of you that he sees, or is he a reaction to that image?

KRISHNAMURTI: Of course, he is the reaction to that image.

Questioner (1): And therefore he is the observed, because of that reaction.

KRISHNAMURTI: You understand?

Questioner (2): Could you explain this a little more?

KRISHNAMURTI: (to first questioner): Would you explain it Sir?

Questioner (1): Well if you ask me to say something, I will.

KRISHNAMURTI: Go ahead Sir, we asked. You stand up, or come here—whatever you like.

Questioner (1): The speaker uses the words, that it is seen that the observer is the observed. Now we have been talking about things that are observed. A tree, that is the observed. Does the speaker mean that awareness sees that I am that tree? No. He says that what I see is not the tree, I see an image of the tree. So, therefore does he mean that I, as the observer, am that image of the tree, or does he mean that I as the observer am the reaction to that image of the tree? That was my question.

KRISHNAMURTI: That's right Sir. You are the reaction to the image which you have created about that tree. If you had no image about that tree there would be no observer.

Questioner: Sir, could one express this a little differently and say that the images that are built by like and dislike through innumerable associations about everything have also built up some conglomerate aggregate that has formed the observer? Now, when we understand this inwardly, without trying to understand it, but are simply aware of it. . . .

KRISHNAMURTI: That's right Sir! That's perfectly right.

Questioner: . . . . then you ask, what happens?

KRISHNAMURTI: Now I'm going into it.

Questioner: Yes, then continue.

KRISHNAMURTI: I'm going on. This awareness has revealed that the observer is the observed, therefore any action on the part of the observer only creates another image— naturally! If the observer has not realized that the observer is the observed, any movement on the part of the observer creates other series of images, and again he's caught in it. So what takes place? When the observer is the observed, the observer doesn't act at all. Go slowly Sir, go very slowly, because it's a very complex thing that we're going into now. I think this must be very clearly understood otherwise we shan't go any further. The observer has always said, "I must do something about these images," "I must get rid of them, I must suppress them, I must transform them, I must give them a different shape." The observer has always been active with regard to the observed. Right? I observe that I dislike my wife—for various reasons—and the observer says, I mustn't dislike her, I must do something about it, and so on. The observer is always active with regard to the thing observed. Right Sir?

Questioner: You mean that we are reacting all the time with all these images, constantly, in terms of like and dislike, and adding to them; that we are always doing this?

KRISHNAMURTI: That's right; and this action of like and dislike on the part of the observer is called positive action.

Questioner: And that's what you mean when you say it is always active.

KRISHNAMURTI: Yes; it is what is called positive action. I like, therefore I must hold or I don't like, therefore I must get rid of it. It's reacting, either passionately or casually. But when the observer realizes that the thing about which he is acting is himself. . . . What Sir?

Questioner: The gentleman over there wanted some more clarity on the observer and the observed. Now what you said then was that these images are not the actual things themselves; you don't know what they are, you only react to these images continuously. And when we see that, then this conflict between the observer and the observed ceases...

248

KRISHNAMURTI: Sir, keep it very simple. I look at that brown shirt and the scarf. If I say, "I don't like that brown shirt and the scarf," or, "I like that brown shirt and the scarf," I've already created an image, which is a reaction.

Questioner: And that stores up in the past, in memory.

KRISHNAMURTI: That's right, that's right. Now, can I look at that brown shirt and the scarf without like and dislike, which is not to react to it but merely to observe? Then there is no image. You've got it, Sir? Have you got that very simple thing?

Questioner: (inaudible)

KRISHNAMURTI: Look Sir, I see somebody has got a red shirt or a red blouse, I look at it. My immediate reaction is: I like or dislike. The like and dislike is the result of my culture, of my training, of my tendency, my inclination, which has already an image which says, "I don't like that shirt," or "I like that shirt." So, the like and dislike and the past training—culture, inherited tendency—all that, has created the image. That is my central observer, that is the observer put together by dislike and so on. That observer is always separate from the thing he observes—obviously; and this awareness has revealed that the observer is the observed. Right?

Questioner: The thing observed—do you mean by that the image that the mind built up? . . . .

KRISHNAMURTI: That's right, that's right. You've got it. Then when the observer is the observed image, then there is no conflict between himself and the image. He is that! He is not separate from that. Before, he was separate and took action about it, did something about it, reacted to it.

249

But when the observer realizes he is *that*, there is no like or dislike. Sir, don't—you examine yourself Sir.

Questioner: The observer is creating all the other images. ...

KRISHNAMURTI: No! I'm not going to go back into that, Sir. We have gone into it sufficiently. You understand what we have said so far, that between the observer and the observed, between the image which the observer has created about himself and the images which he has created about various things there is a separation, a division, and hence, between himself and them, there is a conflict of like and dislike and reaction. And he is always doing something about it. Now, when the observer realizes he is the observed—the images—then conflict ceases. That is, when I realize I am fear—not, that there is fear and me separate from that fear—then I am that fear; I can't do anything. Follow this closely. Because, what am I to do? I am part of that fear. I am not separate from fear. Therefore I can look at that fear without any form of escape. I am that fear, I am that pain which I have now in the tummy, or in my leg, or whatever it is. I am that fear. So I don't rebel against it or accept it or run away from it—it is there! So all action, which is the outcome of the reaction of like and dislike, has come to an end. All right—you follow? Now what has happened?

Questioner: There's only awareness.

KRISHNAMURTI: No.

Questioner: There is neither the observer nor the observed.

KRISHNAMURTI: That's it. There is an awareness which is becoming more and more—I'm using more and more not in the sense of time—more and more acute, sharp, intense.

250

Questioner: Not wasting energy.

KRISHNAMURTI: That's right. It's becoming tremendously alive, it is not bound to any central issue, or to any image. And it is becoming intensely aware; from that intensity there comes a different quality of attention. Right?

Questioner: And this intensity, Sir, has no direction and no purpose.

KRISHNAMURTI: Watch it Sir, you don't have to ask me. Watch it yourself. The moment there is a choice in this awareness, then there is a direction directed by this observer. Right? But when the whole pattern, when this whole structure has been understood, conflict has come to an end; and therefore the mind—because the mind is this awareness—has become extraordinarily sensitive, highly intelligent. Because sensitivity goes with intelligence—there is no intelligence without sensitivity, physical as well as psychological—the mind has become highly intelligent and sensitive! Because that intelligence is not put together by any conflict. There is the intelligence which has been put together through conflict, which is the observer. The observer separate from the observed has its own intelligence. I don't want to go into that.

In this awareness, because it has exposed everything very clearly, there has been no choice (choice only exists when there is confusion) and so this awareness has removed every form of conflict; therefore there is clarity. And this clarity is attention. Don't agree please! This requires actual *doing*, not just agreeing. When there is this attention, in which there is no observer nor observed, this attention *is* intelligence. In this attention there is no conflict whatsoever, therefore there is no demand for *anything*! And, this attention has its own activity, its own action. So there is an action which is not born out of the observer. When the observer acts, his action is always separate. Sir, look. We cannot go further into this matter unless you have actually

251

done it—actually do it. Then you will find that attention, being intelligence, is beauty and love—which the observer, separate, tries to imitate—then the mind has no limit.

7th August 1967

THE CONCISE COLUMBIA ENCYCLOPEDIA

THE COLUMBIA UNIVERSITY PRESS

A new, comprehensive, and authoritative, one-volume encyclopedia of biographies, facts and information for everyday use in the 80's. Written under the guidance of a distinguished panel of scholars in every field. THE CONCISE COLUMBIA ENCYCLOPEDIA is the product of years of careful research and planning to make an encyclopedia's worth of information available in one volume which is small enough to take anywhere!

- Over 15,000 entries covering every field of information
- Over 3,000 articles on up-to-date scientific and technical subjects—from computers to robotics and quarks
- Broad coverage of people and topics of contemporary importance—from Sandra Day O'Connor and Luciano Pavarotti to genetic engineering and herpes simplex
- Over 5,000 biographies of notable men and women, past and present
- Illustrations, diagrams, charts, national and regional maps
- A 16-page world atlas of political and topographical maps
- Over 50,000 cross references to additional information
- Pronunciation guide for difficult names and words
- Metric equivalents for all measurements
- Plus special tables listing U.S. presidents, Supreme Court justices, popes, prime ministers, rulers, royal dynasties, national parks, theaters, orchestras, languages, planets, elements—and much more!

An AVON Trade Paperback   63396-5/$14.95